HOYLE'S
RULES OF
GAMES

HOYLE'S RULES OF GAMES

THIRD UPDATED AND REVISED EDITION

Descriptions of Indoor Games of Skill and
Chance, with Advice on Skillful Play.
Based on the Foundations laid down by
Edmond Hoyle, 1672–1769.

EDITED BY ALBERT H. MOREHEAD
AND GEOFFREY MOTT-SMITH

REVISED AND UPDATED BY PHILIP D. MOREHEAD

ABRIDGED VERSION EDITED BY CARA ELY

A SIGNET BOOK

SIGNET
Published by New American Library, a division of
Penguin Putnam Inc., 375 Hudson Street,
New York, New York 10014, U.S.A.
Penguin Books Ltd, 80 Strand,
London WC2R ORL, England
Penguin Books Australia Ltd, Ringwood,
Victoria, Australia
Penguin Books Canada Ltd, 10 Alcorn Avenue,
Toronto, Ontario, Canada M4V 3B2
Penguin Books (N.Z.) Ltd, 182–190 Wairau Road,
Auckland 10, New Zealand

Penguin Books Ltd, Registered Offices:
Harmondsworth, Middlesex, England

Published by Signet, an imprint of New American Library,
a division of Penguin Putnam Inc.

First Signet Printing, Second Revised Edition, September 1983
First Signet Printing, Third Revised and Updated Edition, December 2001
First Special Sales Printing, August 2002. ISBN: 0-451-20846-3
10 9 8 7 6 5 4 3 2 1

Game title illustrations by Tim Grajek.
Not for Resale

CONTENTS

BACKGAMMON

BACKGAMMON (called TRICTRAC in some countries, and in ancient times called Tables) is probably thousands of years older than Chess. Together with Pachisi (Parcheesi) it probably evolved from the practice of scoring the rolls of dice by moving a token along a track. About 1925 Backgammon spurted into new popularity in the United States, due probably to the introduction of the doubling rule, which gave added scope for skill as well as "pepping up" the tempo of play. It is now enjoying a period of wide popularity.

Backgammon is played by two, on a special board with pieces resembling checkers. Each player is provided with fifteen pieces, also with two dice and a dice cup from which to cast them. The players are conventionally called Black and White, though their pieces may be of any two contrasting colors, dark and light.

THE BOARD. The Backgammon board is divided into two halves or *tables* by a center partition called *the bar*. (See diagram.) The board is conventionally placed so that the inner table is "toward the light." In each table are twelve *points*, which in the illustration are numbered for reference. (The

1

numbers are not printed on the actual board.) The illustration
shows how the pieces are set up to commence a game.

THE PLAY. The moves are governed by casting dice. Each
player has two dice, and usually a dice cup. To begin a
game, each player rolls one die, and the higher number
plays first. If the numbers are the same, both players must
roll again. The first player uses the numbers on the two
dice as his first roll. (Some play that he starts with a fresh
roll of his own two dice.) After that the turn alternates,
and each player casts his own two dice to determine what
he can do.

The object of play is to be the first to move all one's
stones (as the pieces are called) into one's inner (or *home*)
table, and thence to continue as though moving them in
the same direction and off the board. The stones move
from point to point, and each player heads toward his own
1-point. White moves from left to right from Black's 1-
point (B1) through Black's 12-point (B12), then through
W12 toward W1. Black moves in the opposite direction,
W1 . . . W12, B12 . . . B1.

THE MOVES. Stones are advanced across a number of points corresponding to the numbers on the dice. Both numbers may be applied to move one stone, or may be applied separately to two stones. For example, if Black has first turn and his roll is 5-4, he can move one stone from W1 to W10, or one from W12 to B8 and another from the same point to B9.

Whenever a player rolls a double number, he takes that number not twice but four times. For example, on a roll of 3-3 the player makes four moves of 3 each, or a move of 3 and another of 9, etc. He moves a total of 12 points, not 6.

When two or more numbers are applied to one stone, the stone must be able to make the two moves consecutively. A stone may not land on a point occupied by two or more of his opponent's stones. For example, with 5-5 Black cannot bring a man from W1 to W11; it is true that he can put a stone on W11, but he cannot move from W1 with a 5 because the White stones on W6 prevent him from landing there.

A stone may jump over adverse stones. For example, Black with a 5-4 may move from W1 to W10 by playing first W1-W5 and then W5-W10. The five White stones on W6 are not a barricade.

A player must use both numbers of his roll (or all four of a doublet) if possible. There are times when a player could advantageously refuse to move, yet he must move in turn if he can. If he can use one number but not the other, he must use the higher number if possible. For example, if the roll is 6-5, and the player can move 6 or 5 but not both, he must move 6.

CLOSED POINTS. Any number of stones of the same color may stay on one point. If there are more than five, they are piled two or three high, to avoid encroaching on the opponent's side of the board. A point occupied by two or more men is *closed* (or *made*); a point occupied by only one man, or none, is *open*. But stones of opposite color may not stay on the same point.

BLOTS. A single stone on a point does not prevent an adverse stone from landing there. The single stone is a *blot*, and an adverse stone can land there with a *hit*. The blot is then picked up and placed on the bar. It must be *entered* before the owner may make any other move.

From the bar, a stone must enter in the adverse home table, upon an open point whose number has been cast on one of the dice. For example, if Black has a stone on the bar and rolls 5-2, he may enter on W2 or W5, whichever, if either, is open. If there is an opposing blot on the point of entry, the entering man hits it and sends it to the bar.

A compound roll will not serve for entry. For example, if the only point open in the White home table is the 5-point, Black could not enter on a roll of 4-1 or 3-2.

Until the stone enters, a player with a stone on the bar may make no other move. If his roll does not permit entry, the turn passes. If the adverse home table is entirely closed (this is called a *shutout*), he does not even roll in turn, but waits until a point of entry is opened. But, having entered, if the player has no other man on the bar he may use the rest of his roll to move any man. Thus, having a man on the bar, a player rolls 5-2; if he enters on the 2, he may now use the 5 to move any stone, including the one he just entered.

BEARING OFF. At any time when all his stones remaining on the board are in his own home table, a player may *bear off*. Bearing off consists of removing the stones from the board, never to return in that game. A stone may be borne off a point whose number shows on either die. For example, if Black rolls 4-3, he may remove a stone from B4 and another from B3. Instead of bearing off, a player may use the numbers to move inside the inner table. For example, on a roll of 5-5 Black might move four stones from B6 to B1.

When a number is rolled higher than the highest point on which the player has any stones left, he must bear off a stone from the outermost occupied point. For example, if Black rolls 6-2 and has no stone on B6, he must bear off B5, or B4 if there is none on B5, etc. But note that a player may always use the numbers in either order. For example, suppose that Black has two stones on B1 and one on B5, while White has a stone on the bar. Black rolls 6-2, and if he bears off two men he will leave a blot on B1. He may avoid blotting by moving first B5-B3, using the 2, then bearing off B3, using the 6.

Since a player *must* use his roll if he can, he must bear off, if he cannot move within his home board, whenever all his stones are in his home board. If, after he has started to bear off, he is hit, he must enter the stone and bring it around the board to his home table, before he can resume bearing off.

GAMMON AND BACKGAMMON. The game ends when either player bears off his last stone. If the loser has borne off at least one stone, and has no stone left in the winner's inner table, he loses a single game. But if he has not borne off a single stone, he loses double for *gammon*, or if, in addition, he has a stone left in the adverse inner table or on the bar, he loses triple for *backgammon*.

DOUBLING. In modern Backgammon, the value of the game may be further increased by voluntary *doubling*. Either may make the first double of a game, just before his turn to roll the dice. Thereafter, the right to double alternates. When a player says "I double," the other must either play on for a double game, or resign and lose the current value of the game. The doubles are cumulative, so that the base value of the game may become 2, 4, 8, 16, etc., before the game ends. The double for gammon and triple for backgammon apply in addition to whatever voluntary doubles have been made. (It is often wise to agree to a limit on the number of voluntary doubles per game, making the base value at most 16, or 32.)

Some players also allow automatic doubles—one for each time that the cast for first play results in like numbers on the two dice. The number of automatic doubles is usually limited by agreement to one or two.

STRATEGY OF BACKGAMMON

In the following discussion of principles, Black is assumed to have won the first turn.

Certain opening rolls are often called *naturals* because

they allow very desirable moves. There is no argument as to the following:

 Move "Lover's Leap," WI-W12, getting one *runner* to the "comfort station."

 Move W12-B7 and B8-B7, making your *bar point*.

 Move B8-B4 and B6-B4, making your 4-point.

 Move B8-B5 and B6-B5, making your 5-point.

As to all other rolls, there are different schools of thought. Here are some of the ideas:

If a runner is to be brought out of the adverse inner table early in the game, it should get as near as possible to the comfort station (W12). Rolls of 6-4, 6-3, 5-4 may be played by B1-B11 or to B10. Shorter leaps, to the 9-point or the bar, are generally avoided as placing the blot where it is too easy to hit.

It is desirable to make one's 5-point and bar-point as quickly as possible. "Builders" should be brought down into the outer table from the comfort station, to assist in making these points. Rolls of 4-3 and 3-2 may well be used to bring two builders down, to B9 and B10 or to B10 and B11 respectively. Rolls of 5-3 and 5-2 are often used the same way, although one of the stones lands on the already-made 8-point. An alternative with 5-3 is to make the 3-point, by B8-W3 and B6-B3.

Putting a blot on the 5-point, hoping to cover it on the next turn, is a worthwhile risk. The classical move for roll of 6-2 is W12-B5. The rolls 5-1, 4-1, 2-1 may be used by moving B6-B5 and bringing down a stone from the comfort station.

Some advocate splitting the *runners* (the two stones on the opponent's 1-point) early, so as to give a chance to make a more advanced point there or to carry the foremost runner clear to the comfort station. With the rolls 4-5, 1-5, 4-3, 3-2, the first number may be used to advance a runner and the second to bring down a builder.

An early doublet should be played as follows, if possible. Each move is made by two stones together.

Move Wl-W7 and W12-B7, making both bar points.

Move W12-B3. If you have already made your 3-point, try to absorb the roll entirely by bringing two stones down from W12 to B8 and moving a stone B6-B1 if White has split his runners.

There is large choice. K12-B5 is much played. A similar idea (making points in the home table) is B8-B4, combined with B6-B2 or W12-B9. Two of the numbers are usually used for WI-W5 if White has made his bar point, or if the numbers cannot all be used to make new points in the home table.

 Move B6-B3 and B8-B5. Having made either point already, use the whole roll for W12-B7. To play W1-W4 or Wl-W7 is usually a waste of good numbers that could better be used elsewhere, if only by W12-B10.

Move B6-B4 and W12-B11. If you have already made your 4-point, choose according to circumstances among Wl-W5, W12-B9, B6-B2.

Move B6-B5 and B8-B7. This roll is the "gambler's dream," as it makes the two strongest points in one turn.

The normal policy in early play is to leave the runners alone (unless they can be brought out on good rolls, such as 6-5, 6-6, 4-4, or by hitting an adverse blot) and to make points around the bar on your side of the table, especially the 5-point and bar point. Bring down builders freely from your comfort station for this purpose. Take risks, as by blotting on your 5-point, while the adverse inner table is still wide open for entry.

Although the 2-point is too remote from the bar to be worth making on a first roll of 6-4, and some players consider it poor to make the 3-point with an early 5-3, once you have made your 4-point or 5-point, *any* additional point in your home table is worth making.

If the opponent leaves a blot on your 5-point, hit it if possible, even at the cost of leaving a blot there which may be hit in turn. If your opponent advances one runner by a short step, to your 4-point, 5-point, or bar point, you should usually smack it if you can, trusting that you can cover your own blot before it is hit. Out of this "wide open" play come *primes*—a barrier of six adjacent points, past which the opponent cannot move. Once you make a prime, you have got to be extremely unlucky to lose the game.

Of course you must play less and less "wide open" as your opponent builds up his home table, making it more difficult for you to enter if you are hit.

Example Game:

Black moves first. The symbol x indicates a hit, and e
means "enters."

	BLACK		WHITE
ROLL	MOVE	ROLL	MOVE

BLACK

ROLL	MOVE
1	4-1 W12-B9. B6-B5.
2	5-3. eW5. B8-B5x.

Playing "wide open"
in the effort to make
one of the 5-points.

| 3 | 6-5 W5-B9. |
| 4 | 5-4 B6-Blx. B9-B5. |

Hoping to keep White
busy so that he cannot
cover W4.

| 5 | 3-2 eW2. W1-W4x. |

| 6 | 4-1 W12-B9. B6-B5. |
| 7 | 6-2 W4-W12. |

Worth consideration is
W2-W4 and W12-B7.
But B7 is depreciated in
value by the fact that
White can escape from
B4 with sixes.

| 8 | 5-1 W12-B12x-B7. |
| 9 | 6-3 W12-B7. B12-B10. |

Now threatening to
make a prime. The
blot is put on B10 be-
cause if White gets a
six Black would like to
be hit, for unless so de-
layed he may soon
have to break up his
blockade.

WHITE

ROLL	MOVE
	4-3 Bl-B5x. B12-W10.
	6-2 eB2. W10-W4.

The blot is brought inside,
where it is a little harder
to hit and easier to cover.

| | 3-1 W8-W5. W6-W5. |
| | 6-1 eBlx. B12-W7. |

Since a blot must be left
somewhere, a builder is
brought down.

| | 4-2 eB4. B2-B4. |

Making it harder for Black
to build up his board.

| | 5-1 B12-W7. |
| | 2-2 W6-W4(2). B12-W9. |

Now if W9 can be covered,
White will have a prime.

| | 4-2 eB4. Bl-B3. |
| | 5-1 W9-W4. B3-B4. |

|---|---|---|---|
	BLACK			WHITE	
ROLL	MOVE		ROLL	MOVE	
10	4-2	B10-B6. Wl-W3.	6-2	B4-B12.
11	3-3	W12-B7. B6-B3. B5-B2.	5-2	B12-W6.
12	2-1	B3-Bl. W2-W3. A lifesaver!	5-4	W6-Wl. W5-Wl. White is not so lucky!
13	4-4	B9-B1 (2).	3-2	W5-W2. W4-W2.
14	6-4	W3-B12.	4-2	W7-W3x-Wl.
15	6-1	Miss.	5-1	B4-B9. W7-W6.
16	4-3	eW3. B12-B8.	6-3	B9-W7.
17	3-1	B8-B5. B7-B6.	6-1	B4-B10. W7-W6.
18	5-5	B8-B3 (2). B7-B2 (2).	4-3	B4-B8. B10-W12. The stone must vacate B4 at once. If Black rolls an ace or deuce, he will surely hit on B4.
19	6-4	W3-B12.	4-2	B8-B12x. W6-W4. He must hit, for Black is ahead in a running game.
20	5-4	eW5. B6-B2.	6-5	W12-W6. B12-W8.
21	5-2	W5-W12.		

Now it is a running game, with the chances about even.

Snake

Snake is an odd way of setting up the stones for a regular Backgammon game. The Black stones are set up as usual: five on B6, three on B8, five on W12, and two on W1. White has only six stones on the board, two each on B1, B2, B3, the other nine being on the bar. All other rules are as in Backgammon.

The advantage in this game probably lies with Black, but the White side is easier to play in the beginning. White has a clear objective—to enter his stones, hit blots and gain time to form a *prime*, then walk his prime around the board until it becomes a *shutout*, trapping one or more Black stones on the bar. Even if Black has begun bearing off before these stones are trapped, he stands to lose unless he has borne off more than five or six stones.

WHITE

BLACK

A *prime*, the occupation of six adjacent points, forms a barrier that adverse stones cannot hurdle. It is *walked* forward by the aid of the three extra stones. A stone is laid, as a blot, just ahead of the prime, and then is covered from the rearmost point of the prime on roll of a 6. If the stone trapped by the prime hits this forward blot, the stone is simply entered and brought around again to the same position. This is the ideal picture of the walking prime, but it may be shattered by untimely doublets, 5-5 or 4-4. Nevertheless, once the prime is formed, the opponent cannot well accept a voluntary double.

The objective for Black is fairly clear, but more difficult to realize in the early stages. If Black tries to bring all his stones into his home board in a hurry, on three points at most, he is likely to have to leave a blot sooner or later. White will vacate the 2-point or 3-point to force blotting when Black rolls a 4 or a 3. To avoid the hazards of such an ending, Black should try in the earliest stages to *split the White forces*. He should maintain a blockade of three or four points outside his bar so long as possible, hoping that White will have to enter all his stones, then take some out from the 3-point on 5s and 6s.

Snake poses in an extreme form the problems that arise in regular Backgammon when one player goes for a *back game*. Having suffered several hits, and thus being far behind in time, a player may decide to "go to the whole hog" and get as many runners into the adverse home table as possible. Tyro Backgammon players are apt to assist rather than hinder an opponent bent on a back game, by hitting too many blots.

Dutch Backgammon

Dutch Backgammon commences with all the stones on the bar. A player must enter all fifteen stones before making any other move, and he may not hit a blot until he has brought at least one stone around to his home table. Here the strategy is to hold three or four of the highest points in the adverse inner table so long as possible, forcing the opponent eventually to place some stones "out of play" on the lower points.

A player who is convinced that he does not get his share of high rolls at regular Backgammon—and it is astonishing how many persons are so ill-favored—should play Dutch Backgammon, for here during most of the game the advantage lies with the player rolling lower numbers.

Acey Deucey

Acey Deucey is an elaboration of Dutch Backgammon, very popular in the U.S. Navy.

No stones are placed on the board at the outset. The players roll for first turn as usual, but the high player casts both his dice for his first roll. A roll may be used to enter additional stones or to move those already entered: moving does not have to wait until all fifteen are on the board, but a player may not move so long as a stone which has been hit is still on the bar. Blots may be hit at any time, and when hit must be entered before the owner may make any other move. All other rules follow regular Backgammon, except for special privileges accorded the roll of 2-1. Having moved the 2-1, the player may then name any doublet he chooses, move accordingly, and then roll the dice again. If unable to use any part of the roll, the player loses the rest. For example, if he can move 2 but not 1 he does not get the doublet or the second turn.

There are many local variations as to doubles and settlement. Some make an automatic double on every roll 2-1, allowing voluntary doubles also. Some allow no automatic doubles, and the loser must pay 1 unit of the stake for every stone he has left on the board, or pay for each remaining stone according to the number of points needed to bear it off. Some eliminate the traditional doubles and triples for gammon and backgammon.

Russian Backgammon

Russian Backgammon differs from all other variants in that both players enter their stones in the same table and move in the same direction around the board to the same home table. No stones are placed on the board at the outset. After entering two stones, the player is free to use subsequent rolls either to enter more stones or to move those already on the board. Blots are hit in the usual way and must be duly entered before the owner may make any other move. Doublets are used twice over, as in regular Backgammon, but then the player also moves in accordance with the complementary doublets. The complement of a number is its difference from 7. For example, having rolled 4-4, the player moves four 4s and four 3s. Of course, if he cannot absorb all the 4s he may not take any 3s. When he can use all eight numbers, he rolls again.

A feature of the strategy is to establish and maintain blockades of three or four adjacent points ahead of the opponent, so as to make it impossible for him to use a doublet.

CHECKERS

CHECKERS *is so called only in the United States. In England and the British dominions it is* DRAUGHTS. *In the Romance and Germanic languages its name is based on Dam (woman); in early times it was deprecated as "women's chess." But it has proved to be as profound, in some respects, as Chess. The nature of Checkers suggests that it had a common ancestor with Chess and Mill, but it has not been traced with certainty earlier than the 14th century. The first scientific treatise on the game was written by Peter Mallet, a French mathematician, Paris, 1668. In the 19th century the game was extensively analyzed and popularized by a great galaxy of English and Scottish players.*

PLAYERS. Checkers is played by two, on the same board that is used for Chess, with pieces (called *checkers* or *draughts*) in the form of thick discs. All the checkers are alike in form but are provided in two colors, the darker being used by the player "Black" and the lighter by "White."

THE BOARD. As in Chess, the board is so placed that each player has a light square in the corner at his right. (In printed diagrams, the apparent colors are reversed. The squares printed dark represent the actual light squares; the actual dark squares are left blank so that numbers and pieces may be printed on them.) For reference purposes, the 32 dark squares are considered to be numbered as shown in the diagram.

THE PIECES. Each player has 12 pieces of his own color. To begin a game, they are placed on the board as shown in the diagram. All the pieces stand and move solely on the dark squares. At the outset, all pieces are *single men*. A single man may later become a *king*, as explained below.

THE PLAY

Black moves first, and thereafter the players move alternately. A player loses the game if he cannot move in turn; usually this is because all his pieces have been captured, but it can also come about because all his remaining pieces are immobilized. Many games are drawn by agreement, when few pieces remain and neither player has an advantage sufficient to win.

NONCAPTURING MOVE. A single man may move only forward on the dark diagonal, one square at a time (when not capturing). For example, Black can make any of the following first moves: 9-13, 9-14, 10-14, 10-15, 11-15, 11-16, 12-16. (A move is denoted by the number of the square moved from and the square moved to.)

CAPTURING MOVE. The capturing move is a jump. If a White piece stands adjacent and forward to a Black piece (e.g., B on 15, W on 18), and if the square back of the White piece on the same line (22) is vacant, the Black piece jumps over it to the vacant square (22), and then the White piece is removed from the board.

If a piece makes a capture, and then is on a square from

which it can jump over another adverse piece, it continues jumping in the same turn. It may change direction during a series of jumps (but only forward). For example, B on 4, W on 8, 16, 24; Black jumps 4-11-20-27.

When able to capture, a player *must* do so; he may not make a noncapturing move. (Under the traditional rule of "huff or blow," if a player violates this rule his opponent may remove from the board the piece that should have made a capture. This rule is still printed in some books, but modern tournament regulations have abolished it. When the rule is violated, the player must retract his illegal move and make the capture instead.)

It sometimes happens that a piece may capture in either of two directions, or either of two pieces may make a capture. In all such situations, the owner has free choice.

CROWNING. The row of squares farthest from the player (1 to 4 for W and 29 to 32 for B) is his *king row*. On reaching the king row, a single man is *crowned* and becomes a *king*. The opponent must immediately put on top of it another piece of the same color, and the two checkers are then moved as a unit.

The king has the same powers as a single man, plus the right to move backward as well as forward. Moves in both directions may be combined in one series of jumps. But if a single man reaches the king row by a capture, it may not continue jumping in the same turn (as a new king); it must pause one turn to be crowned.

STRATEGY OF CHECKERS

Many volumes of analysis have been published without exhausting Checkers. Here, space permits us to state only some pointers useful to beginners.

An expert once said, "Checkers is an easy game. All you have to do is to avoid losing pieces." Then he added, "Of course, the average Checker player can be depended on to fall into a two-for-one shot before he has made a dozen moves." For example, Black opens 11-15 and White answers 22-17. Black plays 12-16, thinking to go on to 20, but White plays 24-19, forcing 15-24, 28-12, and White has won a piece. Another way to do the same thing is 9-14, 22-17, 12-16, 23-18, 14-23, 26-12. The first thing a beginner has to do is to learn to avoid such simple two-for-one shots, which abound.

The loss of a single piece is normally enough to lose the game. The opponent can usually swap piece for piece and so end up with one-to-none. There are some end positions, however, where one piece can draw against two, and sometimes the sacrifice of a piece is correct because it can ultimately be regained.

A king is particularly powerful behind adverse single men, where it can attack without suffering counterattack. Therefore in the opening it is important not to let an avenue to your king row be opened up to the adverse pieces, unless you can also crown. Many a game is won by the first king. Forcing too many *cuts* (exchanges of captures) in the opening is one easy way to let the enemy through.

All these points are illustrated by the following example game. (Read down the columns.)

Example Game:

11-15	14-17	17-21	18-15 (k)	23-27
23-19	21-14	19-15	19-16	15-19
9-14	10-17	22-25	5-9	27-31 (n)
27-23 (a)	18-14 (e)	15-8	7-2	19-24 (o)
8-11	17-22	4-11	10-14* (1)	14-18
22-18	26-17	28-24	2-7	20-16
15-22	13-22	25-29	3-10	18-23
25-9	28-24 (f)	24-19	16-11	24-28 (p)
5-14	2-6	29-25	15-8	31-27
29-25	32-28 (g)	31-26 (i)	12-3	28-32
6-9	12-16 (h)	7-10	14-18	27-24
25-22	19-12	26-22 (j)	3-7	16-11
9-13	6-10	11-15	10-14	24-19
24-20 (b)	23-18	18-11	7-11 (m)	11-7
1-5 (c)	10-17	25-18	18-23	19-15
22-18 (d)	24-19	11-7	11-15	7-2
				15-10 (q)

(a) The Defiance opening.

(b) Not good is 22-18, for after 14-17, 21-14, 10-17 Black threatens to break through and crown on 29.

(c) Other options here are 11-15 and 4-8.

(d) Now playable because Black has opened his king row.

(e) There is a safe draw by 26-22.

(f) This move and the next are dictated by the precarious position of the man on 14, which Black threatens to win by 2-6 and 6-10.

(g) Now if 6-10, then 14-9, 5-14, 23-18, 14-23, 19-16, 12-19, 24-6. White will make a king and regain his piece.

(h) Yates sprang this surprise move on Wyllie in 1876. The point of it is that the man on 14 is won and Black crowns quickly.

(i) Useless is 19-15, for then 25-22, 15-8, 22-15 and Black holds three White men with two.

(j) Of course not 19-16, 10-15, winning two for one.

(k) Thus Black gets the bind after all: The king and the man on 3 hold the three White men.

(l) 9-14 would actually lose after 2-6. But now Black threatens to make two more kings and use them to bottle up the White king. White's only chance is to sacrifice a piece in the hope of regaining it by attack on the Black single men. The star means the move is the only one that will win (or, in some cases, draw).

(m) He cannot play 7-10 because of 9-13.

(n) If 27-32, to keep White out of the double corner, then 19-23 and will threaten eventually to lock up the three Black men with two pieces.

(o) Useless is 19-23, 31-26, 23-19, 26-22.

(p) So as to meet 23-27 with 28-32.

(q) White cannot regain his piece, and the extra man wins.

CRIBBAGE

CRIBBAGE *is believed to have been invented and christened by the English poet Sir John Suckling, who lived 1609-1642. Some of its features were taken from an older game, Noddy, of which little is known. Early colonists brought Cribbage to America, where it flourishes.*

PLAYERS. Two. Adaptation can be made for three or four.

CARDS. A regular pack of 52. The cards rank: K (high), Q, J, 10, 9, 8, 7, 6, 5, 4, 3, 2, A. The suits play little part; the cards are used chiefly as numbers. Each face card represents 10, each ace 1, each other card its index value. Face cards and tens are called "tenth cards."

THE DEAL. Each player receives six cards, dealt one at a time.

THE CRIB. From his hand each player selects two cards, and the four cards are placed face down near the dealer. They form the *crib*, an extra hand that belongs to the dealer.

THE STARTER. After the crib is laid away, the nondealer cuts the rest of the pack, and the dealer turns up the top card of the lower portion. This card is the *starter*. If it is a jack, the dealer *pegs* (scores) 2 points.

THE CRIBBAGE BOARD. Scores accrue so rapidly that a special scoring device is used, a *Cribbage board*. As shown in the illustration, the board is an oblong panel having four rows of 30 holes each, plus some extra *game holes* at one end. Each player uses two pegs, which at the outset are placed in the game holes. Each item of score is marked by jumping the rearward peg ahead of the other by a corresponding number of holes. The pegs are marched away from the head of the board (the end with the game holes) along an outer row of holes, then back along an inner row. The game may be played "once around," for a total of 61 points, but far more common is "twice around," for a total of 121.

THE PLAY. In playing his cards, each player retains possession of them, merely exposing them face up in a pile in front of himself.

The nondealer begins by playing any card, announcing its point value, as "Ten" if he leads a face card or ten. Dealer then plays a card, announcing the total of the two cards, as "Seventeen" if he plays a seven. Play continues alternately, the new total being announced each time, until the player in turn is unable to play without carrying the total over thirty-one. He must then say "Go." The other pegs for the *go* (as explained below); then the player who called the go must lead again for a new series of plays. The count begins again at zero, and again the total must not be carried beyond thirty-one.

After go is called, the other must play additional cards if he can do so without exceeding thirty-one. Thus the same player may play two or three times in succession. For making exactly thirty-one the player pegs 2; for a go at less than thirty-one he pegs 1. Playing the last card of all (of the eight in play) counts 1 for last, or 2 if it makes thirty-one.

SCORING IN PLAY. Other points may be scored in play besides the go's. These are as follows:

Fifteen. For making the count fifteen, peg 2.

Pairs. For playing a card of same rank as that just played, peg 2. (Pairing goes by rank, e.g., a king with a king, not with a queen, though both have the point value of 10.) For playing the third card of a rank peg 6, and for playing the fourth peg 12.

Runs. For playing a card that is in sequence of rank with two or more played just previously, peg the number of cards in the *run* (sequence). For example, if the cards played are 4, 6, 5, the last player pegs 3 for run plus 2 for fifteen. The cards need not be played in sequential order to score for run, so long as no foreign cards intervene. For example, if the cards played are 4, K, 6, 5 there is no run.

SHOWING. By *showing* is meant counting and scoring a hand. The hands are shown in strict order: nondealer, dealer's hand, crib.

The starter is treated as a fifth card belonging to each of these three hands. The combinations that score are as follows:

Fifteen. For each combination of cards that total fifteen, score 2. "Combination" here is meant in the strict sense. Thus, a hand (with starter) of 9, 8, 7, 7, 6 has three combinations of fifteen: 9 and 6, 8 with one 7, 8 with the other 7. A hand of J, 5, 5, 5, 5 has no less than eight combinations of fifteen: four of J and 5, four of three 5's. (This hand, when the J also scores as *his nobs*, makes 29, the largest possible score.)

Pairs. For a pair, score 2; for three of a kind (called *pair royal* or "proil"), 6; for four of a kind (*double pair royal*), 12.

Runs. For each combination that makes a run of three or more, peg the number of cards in the run. In the hand 9, 8, 7, 7, 6 there are 8 points for two runs of four, using the 7's in turn.

Flush. For four cards in hand (not crib, and excluding the starter) of the same suit, score 4, or 5 if the starter is also of the same suit. For crib and starter all of the same suit, score 5. (There is no score for a four-flush in the crib.)

His Nobs. For a jack in hand, of same suit as the starter, score 1. The jack scored as starter by dealer is called *his heels.*

Proper etiquette is to count aloud, taking the categories in the order given above, and indicating the source of the scores briefly. For example, in scoring K, K, 10, 5, 4, the player would say "Fifteen two, fifteen four, fifteen six, and a pair makes eight." The opponent must be given time to verify the score. It is proper to announce the scores for certain combinations *in toto*, as pair royal and double pair royal (call "Six" or "Twelve"; do not count the separate pairs). Other standard combinations count as follows for runs and pairs alone (exclusive of fifteens and other items):

Double run, as K, Q, Q, J, scores 8.
Double run of four, as K, Q, Q, J, 10, scores 10.
Triple run, as K, Q, Q, Q, J, scores 15.
Quadruple run, as K, Q, Q, J, J, scores 16.

MUGGINS. If a player overlooks a score to which he is entitled, either in playing or in showing, the opponent may call "Muggins!" and take the score himself. This rule should be waived when a beginner plays against an experienced player.

GAME. When a player pegs into the game hole that gives him 121 (or 61) points, he wins the game forthwith—nothing more is scored. If the loser has not passed the halfway mark—has not reached 61 in "twice around" or 31 in "once around"—he is *lurched* and loses a double game.

IRREGULARITIES IN CRIBBAGE

NEW DEAL. There must be a new deal by the same dealer if a card is exposed in dealing, or if, before nondealer lays away to the crib, it is found that a wrong number of cards was dealt.

WRONG NUMBER OF CARDS. If a player is found (too late for a new deal) to have an incorrect number of cards in his hand, the opponent may either have the hand corrected or may let it stand and peg 2. A short hand is corrected by drawing cards from the stock; a long hand is corrected by discarding cards drawn from it by the opponent. If the crib has the wrong number of cards it must be corrected and nondealer pegs 2.

FAILURE TO PLAY. If a player calls go when able to play, or fails to play when able after opponent calls go, the card or cards he could have played are dead and opponent pegs 2. Dead cards are unplayable; the owner must complete his play with a short hand; but the cards are counted in showing.

ERROR IN SCORING. A player may correct his own error in announcing his score before he has pegged it, but a score once pegged may not be changed except on demand of opponent.

A player may demand correction of an incorrect amount pegged by his opponent, provided that he does so before making his next play, or showing his own hand, or gathering the cards, etc.

STRATEGY OF CRIBBAGE

The choice of cards to give the crib is often easy. Count all the points in the six cards, then lay away the two picked to leave the maximum possible score in the remaining four. But sometimes this course would put points or valuable cards in the crib, so that if the crib is not yours you may do better to deplete your hand somewhat in order to *balk* the crib. Dangerous cards to put in the adverse crib are fives, sevens, and eights, and *near* cards—two in sequence or in sequence-but-one. The best balking cards are very high, very low, and *wide* cards generally—separated in rank by two or more.

Sometimes you are forced to split combinations, even when the crib is yours. As a rule, keep a run of three or more, splitting a pair instead, if necessary. Holding a run gives you maximum chance of increasing your count by help of the starter.

In the play, the main principle is to try to prevent your opponent from making fifteen, or a run, unless you can riposte with a score. Obviously, the safest opening lead is a four, because opponent can then neither make fifteen nor pass fifteen and so deprive you of a chance to make it. (He

might pair your four——but against pairs there is no
defense.)

A card counting ten (ten or face card) is supposed to be a
bad lead, but actually is no more dangerous than a seven,
eight, or any other middle card. In fact, a ten card is a good
lead if you have a five: if your opponent makes fifteen, you
make a pair. Similarly, a lead from two cards that total fifteen
(9 and 6, 7 and 8) is good.

After a lead, the question sometimes arises whether to
play on or *play off*, that is, play a near card making se-
quences possible, or play a wide card. Naturally you should
play on only if you can extend any sequence that your
opponent might make.

When no other considerations supervene, play your high
cards first, saving low cards to eke out a go.

Example Deal

NONDEALER   DEALER

Nondealer lays away 10-3. He cannot keep his entire score,
so saves one sequence combination (8-7) and the valuable
fivespot, with the jack to make a fifteen. He gives the ten
rather than the jack so as to avoid giving *his nobs*.

Dealer has an easy discard, the K-A, saving the double
run. After the starter is turned, the situation is:

NONDEALER   STARTER   DEALER

The play card by card is as follows:

1. Nondealer leads his eight. "Eight." Either the eight or seven should be led, but which one is a guess.

2. Dealer plays the seven. "Fifteen, and two." He pegs 2. He might have made a pair of eights for the same score, but prefers to "play on" by building toward a run.

3. Nondealer plays the seven. "Twenty-two and a pair." Pegs 2.

4. Dealer plays ♦ 9. "Thirty-one." Pegs 2.

5. Nondealer leads the jack. "Ten." On general principle, the lower card is saved as giving a better chance for go.

6. Dealer plays the other nine. "Nineteen." He does not play the eight because nondealer's last card might be an eight. it surely is not a nine, else nondealer on the third play would have made a run of three rather than a pair.

7. Nondealer plays the five. "Twenty-four." Dealer calls "Go," and nondealer pegs 1.

8. Dealer plays the eight. "One for last." Pegs 1.

Nondealer shows as follows: "Fifteen two (J-5), fifteen four (8-7), and a run (8-7-6-5) makes eight." Pegs 8.

Dealer shows his hand: "Fifteen two (8-7), fifteen four (9-6), fifteen six (9-6 using the other nine), and double run of four (counting 10) makes sixteen." Pegs 16. He then turns up the crib. "I have nineteen!" (i.e., no score; for there is no possible hand that counts 19).

Three-Hand Cribbage

Three-Hand Cribbage follows the rules of two-hand except in the following respects: Five cards are dealt to each player, and one card is dealt to the crib. Each player lays away one card to the crib. Eldest hand cuts for the starter and leads first. On a call of go, the other hands must continue to play if able and the last to play scores for the go. The new lead is made by the first to call go. In showing, the order is: eldest hand first, then player at his left, then dealer's hand, finally the crib. Triangular Cribbage boards are made for scoring this game.

Four-Hand Cribbage

Four-Hand Cribbage is played in two partnerships, which may be determined by drawing cards, the two lowest playing against the two highest. Lowest card deals first. Five cards are dealt to each player, of which one is laid away to the crib. Eldest hand cuts for the starter and makes the first lead. On a call of go, the other hands continue to play if able, and the last side to play scores for the go. The new lead is made by the first player to call go. Only one score is kept for each side. In showing, the order is: nondealing side first, then dealer's side, finally the crib, which belongs to dealer's side.

Table Top Cribbage

This variant is for two players sitting next to each other or four people playing as partners. For two players, deal twelve cards to each player, face down, one on top of the other forming a packet. For four players, deal six cards to each. Players must not look at any card before their turn to play. After the deal, the next card is placed face up in the middle of the table and a coin is placed on top of it to mark the center of the layout. The remainder of the deck is out of play. The play consists of playing the dealt cards to form a five-by-five square layout centered on the card with the coin. The player to dealer's left begins and play passes clockwise. At a player's turn he turns up the top card of his stack and places it face up on the layout. It must be played on an empty space, and it must touch at least one card already in the layout, either side to side, end to end, or corner to corner. Cards cannot be played more than two spaces away from the center card, as then they would be outside the limits of the final layout. The cards are turned one at a time.

In the four-player game, partners may confer on where each of their cards should be placed, but in the case of disagreement, the final decision rests with the decision of the player whose turn it is. Players are not allowed to know any of their cards until they are turned up in turn. When all the spaces in the layout are filled, the hand is scored as in Cribbage, except that only 5-card flushes are scored. The partners (or player) facing the ends of the layout (North-South) will score for Cribbage combinations in each of the five columns, while the partners or player facing the sides of the cards (East-West) will score each of the five rows. There is of course no score for heels, nobs, 31, or last. Scores can be pegged on a cribbage board or written on a score pad.

DOMINOES

DOMINOES *are thought to have been derived, in remote times, from dice—perhaps the oldest of all gaming implements. The bones came to be called dominoes from their fanciful resemblance to the style of half-mask called domino.*

GENERAL RULES OF DOMINOES

Dominoes are rectangular tiles marked with all possible combinations of numbers that can be rolled with two dice. There are twenty-one different combinations. But the number zero is always added to the set, by way of "blanks," adding seven more *bones*, as the pieces are called. The widely used domino set contains twenty-eight pieces, the "heaviest" of which is 6-6. Sets are also made that run up to 12-12, containing ninety-one bones, but they are little used.

The bones whose two ends are alike are called *doublets*. Each doublet belongs to one *suit* alone, while every other bone belongs to two suits. In the set up to 6-6, there are seven bones in each suit, but *eight ends* of any one number.

As between two bones, one is *heavier* than the other if it has more dots, the other being *lighter*.

To begin any game, the bones are placed face down on the table and are shuffled by being moved about at random.

Care must be taken not to face any domino in so doing. Each player draws a number of bones at random from this common pile, to form his hand. Dominoes are made thick and heavy enough to stand on edge on the table.

For the first play, a bone is laid face up on the table. All subsequent bones played must be matched with those already down, usually by like numbers on one end of the bone played and an *open end* of the layout. For example, if the first played is the 6-5, the next must have a 6 or a 5 at one end and be placed against the other with like ends touching. An open end of the layout is one on which it is legal to play. The number of open ends varies with the particular game and also with the circumstances. Usually these ends are self-evident, being in fact the ends of various branches, but sometimes new branches may sprout from the sides of old.

One object of a Domino game is invariably to get rid of all the bones in the hand. There may also be scoring in the course of play. The games are of two kinds according to the rule governing the play when a player has no playable bone. In the *block* game, he loses his turn. In the *draw* games, he draws bones from the common stock, called the *boneyard*, until he gets one that he can play.

THE BLOCK GAME

The block game is the simplest of all Domino games. Two, three, or four may play. With two, each player draws seven bones for his hand. With three or four, each takes five bones.

The player holding the highest doublet *sets* it—lays it down as the first play. The turn to play then rotates to his left. Each play is made by adding a bone to an open end of the layout, with like numbers touching. The layout always has two open ends. The two branches are built off the sides of the *set*, and all doublets are customarily placed crosswise, but this does not affect the number of open ends.

If a player cannot play in turn, he passes. The game ends when a player gets rid of his hand or when no player is able to add to the layout. The one with the *lightest* remaining hand (which may be no bones at all) wins the total of pips on all bones remaining in the other hands. The amount needed to win a game may be fixed by agreement, as 100 in three-hand play.

All that a player can do to control his destiny in this simple block game is to try to keep the largest assortment of different numbers in his hand as long as possible. For example, if a player has choice of playing the 5-4 or 5-3 on an open 5, he should choose according as he has other 4s or 3s in his hand.

Tiddly-Wink

Tiddly-Wink is the block game adapted for a large number of players, say six to nine. Each draws only three bones. The player with the highest doublet sets it. There is only one open end on the layout, three sides of the set being forever closed. Bones are played by matching as usual. If unable to play in turn, a player passes. Anyone playing a doublet, including the set, has the right to play a second time, if able. The first hand to "go out" wins, or the lightest hand if play comes to a standstill before any goes out. The winner takes a pool that is formed by equal antes from all players before the draw.

Sebastopol

Sebastopol is in effect a block game because there is no boneyard. Four play, and each draws seven bones. The 6-6 must be set, and the turn then rotates to the left of the first player. The 6-6 is open four ways, and the first four plays after the set must be upon it—no branches may be extended until all four have sprouted. In all other respects the rules are those of the Block Game.

THE DRAW GAME

The Draw Game, at its simplest, follows the rules of the Block Game except that a player having no playable bone must draw from the boneyard until he gets one. After the boneyard is exhausted, a hand unable to play passes. The lightest hand, when play ends in a block or a player goes out, wins the total of points left in all other hands. Game may be fixed at 50 or 100 points.

Bergen

Bergen is a draw game in which the highest doublet is set and the layout always has two open ends. A player scores 2 points for *double-header* if he makes the two ends alike in number, or 3 for *triple-header* if in addition there is a doublet at one end. The winner of a deal scores 1 point. Game is 15 points.

Matador

Matador is a draw game in which adjacent ends on the layout do not match, but total 7. An open 6 calls for a 1, 5 for 2, 4 for 3, and so on. A blank is closed to the play of anything but a *matador*, one of the four bones 0-0, 6-1, 5-2, 4-3. A matador may be played at any time anywhere, without regard to the numbers, and with either end against the layout. Doublets are placed endwise, thus counting singly. For example, 1-1 is playable on a 6, not on a 5.

Sniff

Sniff is one of the best of all Domino games, especially when played by two. It may also be played by three or four. With two, each player draws seven bones for his hand. With three or four, each takes five.

First turn to play is decided by lot, and the leader may play any bone in his hand. As will be seen presently, he may score by his play. Until the first doublet is played, the layout has only two open ends. The first doublet becomes *the sniff*, and is open to play on all four sides.

The object of play is only secondarily to get rid of the hand. Foremost is to score during play. After each play the total of the numbers on the open ends is noted, and when this is a multiple of 5 the player who made it so scores the total (called *muggins* points). For example, if the leader sets the 3-2, he scores 5. If the second hand places the 2-

4, and the third plays the 3-3 crosswise, the latter player scores 10.

Because sniff is open four ways, the first doublet may be played either crosswise or endwise. For example, if the set is 3-2, scoring 5, the next hand may add the 3-3 endwise so as to score 5 also.

Although the layout is open in four directions after sniff is down, there still may be only two or three countable ends, for the sides of sniff do not count in the total until they have sprouted. A doublet other than sniff must be placed crosswise, and both its ends count in the total until it is canceled by the play of another bone on it. If the ends of sniff (as contrasted to the sides) project from the layout, they count even though they have not yet sprouted. For example, if sniff is 5-5, and branches are built off the sides until 6-6 is played on one side, 4-4 on the other, the total is 30.

If unable to play in turn, a player must draw from the boneyard until able. Some make the rule that the last two bones may not be drawn. It is well to have agreement on this point before commencing a game. A player may draw from the boneyard even if able to play without drawing and sometimes it is worthwhile to do so.

The hand that goes out, or has the lightest count if the game ends in a block, wins the total points remaining in the other hands, taken to the nearest multiple of 5. For example, 7 counts as 5 and 8 as 10. In two-hand, the first to reach 200 wins a game. With more players, game may be 200, but usually is lowered to 100 by agreement, for there is less opportunity for scoring *muggins* points (for making the total of open ends a multiple of 5).

STRATEGY OF SNIFF

Certain bones are of intrinsic value because they give greatest probability of making a muggins score. The 5-5, 6-4, 5-0, 4-1, and 3-2 score as the set. The 5-5, 5-0, and 0-0 always make a score if played when the preceding hand has made a score. The 6-1 usually has the same effect. The 6-3, 4-2, 2-1 make a score if played after the previous hand has scored by playing the doublet of the lower number (3-3, 2-2, or 1-1). The bone that matches sniff at one end and has 5 at the other scores if played off a side of sniff after the previous hand has scored.

Especially in two-hand, there is opportunity to save such bones until they can be played to good effect. If the opponent is not too nearly out, it may be worthwhile drawing a few bones to try to avoid having to give up the 5-0 or 6-1 without scoring. Likewise occasion arises for drawing to get a particular bone that will make a score. A player with three or four more bones than his opponent is sometimes able to score in several successive turns, earning more than his investment.

HEARTS

HEARTS *is so called because every card of the heart suit counts "minus" when won in tricks. The object of play is usually the reverse of that in Bridge and other games, where the object is to win certain cards or tricks. Indeed, the 18th-century ancestor of Hearts was called* REVERSE. *The traditional game of Hearts is described first, but other forms such as* BLACK LADY *and* OMNIBUS HEARTS *(described later) have become more popular.*

PLAYERS. Three to six; the best game is four-hand. In every case, each plays for himself.

CARDS. A regular pack of 52. With more or less than four players, discard enough low cards (♣ 2, ♦ 2, ♣ 3, ♠ 2) so that all players have the same number of cards. (Another method is to put any cards remaining after the deal in a separate pile called the *kitty*. The winner of the first trick adds the kitty to his tricks. Some games allow him to look at the kitty, others do not.) In each suit the cards rank: A (high), K, Q, J, 10, 9, 8, 7, 6, 5, 4, 3, 2.

THE DEAL. The whole pack is dealt, one at a time in rotation to the left.

THE PLAY. The player at left of the dealer leads first. (A

common variant is that the player holding the ♣ 2 makes the opening lead with that card.) A player must follow suit to a lead if able; if unable to follow suit, he may play any card. A trick is won by the highest card played on the suit led. The winner of a trick leads to the next. Some also stipulate that hearts (and the ♠ Q in Black Lady) cannot be led until a heart (or the ♠ Q) has been discarded on a trick.

SCORING. All players are provided at the outset with equal numbers of chips. Before each deal, equal antes are put into a pool. After the play, if one player alone is *clear* (has taken no heart), he wins the whole pool. If two are clear, they divide the pool. If all four are *painted* (win hearts), or if all the hearts are taken by one player, the pool is a *jack*; that is, it remains on the table to be won later, increased by the subsequent antes.

IRREGULARITIES IN HEARTS

MISDEAL. It is a misdeal if dealer exposes a card, or gives any hand an incorrect number of cards, or otherwise departs from prescribed procedure. A misdeal may be called at any time before the first trick is completed; otherwise the deal stands as regular. On a proper call of misdeal, the cards are thrown in and redealt by the next dealer (the offender thus losing his turn to deal).

INCORRECT HAND. If at any time after the first trick any hand is found to have an incorrect number of cards, this hand must take all the cards remaining in the hands after the last complete trick is played. If two or more hands are incorrect, these excess cards go to all alike, and each faulty hand is charged with the full number of hearts in the excess cards.

PLAY OUT OF TURN. There is no penalty for a lead or play out of turn, but any player who has not yet played to the trick may demand that it be retracted (in which case any other cards subsequently played must also be retracted). If no player (entitled to do so) demands retraction, the out-of-turn play stands as regular. The owner of an out-of-turn card may not retract it except on proper demand of another player.

REVOKE. If a player fails to follow suit when able, he

may correct his error without penalty before the trick is turned down and quitted. If a revoke is not corrected in time and is discovered before the deal has been scored, the offender is charged for all the hearts in that deal.

STRATEGY OF HEARTS

When the play begins, each hand is intent on avoiding hearts. But once a player has taken a heart, he does not care how many more he may have to take. His only chance at the pool will be to paint every other player or to win all the hearts himself. If two or three are painted, they naturally conspire to paint the others also.

The basis of the play is straight "nullo"—the effort to win no trick, or only harmless tricks. High cards that can be forced to take tricks in three leads of a suit should be played early rather than late. Aces and high cards accompanied by some low cards are not dangerous, but middle cards without low cards are very dangerous. A holding such as Q-9-8 should be led each and every time the opportunity offers, in the effort to dispose of it before cards of this suit are discarded from other hands. A holding such as J-10-9-8-6 is desperately bad and should be discarded whenever opportunity offers, so long as any lower cards of the suit remain unplayed.

Adequately guarded high cards should, however, be saved so long as there is no danger in doing so. Nullo play alone will not suffice if another player has a chance to win all the hearts. A high-card entry sometimes is invaluable in letting a clear hand interrupt a "take-all" to make a killing lead that paints another hand.

Black Lady

See Hearts, page 34, for rules as to Players, Cards, The Deal, The Play, and Irregularities. Black Lady differs only in the following features:

THE BLACK LADY. The ♠ Q is a "minus" card additional to the hearts, counting 13. The focus of play is thus to avoid winning the Black Lady (also called Black Maria or Calamity Jane), the hearts being relatively minor.

In club play this rule is usually adopted: The player holding the ♠ Q must get rid of it on the first trick he can, either by discard or by playing it under the ♠ A or ♠ K already in the trick. The purpose of this rule is to forestall quarrels that may arise from the feeling that favoritism is shown in the disposal of the ♠ Q. But often "favoritism" (in self-interest) is the soul of the strategy.

THE PASS. After the deal is completed, each player must pass any three cards from his hand to his left neighbor. He must select his pass before looking at the cards received from his right neighbor. (*Alternative:* In some circles the rule is to pass alternately to the left and right in successive deals; sometimes there is one deal in each cycle in which no cards are passed.)

TAKE-ALL (also called *shooting the moon*). If a player takes all thirteen hearts and the ♠ Q: (a) there is no score or settlement for the deal; (b) this player scores +26; or (c) all other players score −26.

SCORING. When there is no take-all, the points taken by each player are charged against him in a running total on the score sheet. A session ends at a prefixed time or when one player reaches 100, as agreed. Then each player settles with every other according to the differences of their scores. The simplest way to settle is to total all the scores and divide by the number of players, thus determining the average score. Each player is charged with his difference from the average: those who are above pay the difference, and those who are below collect.

STRATEGY OF BLACK LADY

The most important consideration in selecting cards to pass is to mitigate spade danger. Any high spades (A, K, or Q) in a holding of less than four spades are very dangerous. Usually pass them; except that the ♠ Q is often safer in the hand than out, so that if you are dealt the ♠ Q adequately guarded (three or more others), keep it.

Unguarded high hearts are also unpleasant, since they may capture many minus cards. Pass them if you can afford to do so. High cards in general are not dangerous if accompanied by two or more low cards. A suit as a whole is dangerous if it is long (four or more cards) and contains no low cards, e.g., ♣ Q J 9 8. If you can afford it, pass two or three cards from such a holding.

Every player who does not have "spade trouble" after the pass has an interest in leading spades and should do so. To force out the ♠ Q by spade leads is the best insurance against taking it later by discard.

With two to four diamonds or clubs, having both high cards and low cards, usually play your high cards early, saving your low cards to escape the more dangerous later rounds. The same advice applies to hearts to some degree. If hearts are led through you and you hold ♥ A 7 2, you might risk playing low, but if you hold ♥ A 2, the low play would be folly: put up your ace and take your licking. The outcome to be avoided at all costs is to give up all your exit cards early, whereupon you may be stuck in the lead and forced to win the last five or six tricks.

If the opening lead of the ♣ 2 is employed (see page 77), the player holding that card before the pass should consider whether or not it is important to win the first trick; if so, the card should be passed.

Cancellation Hearts

This is a variant for six or more players. Shuffle together two regular 52-card packs and deal them out as far as they will go evenly. Leave the extra cards face down on the table; these go to the winner of the first trick. The rules are as in Black Lady, plus one added rule: When identical cards (as two jacks of clubs) fall on the same trick, they cancel each other—neither can win the trick. It may happen under this rule that no card in a trick can win it; in such a case, the trick is held aside and goes to the winner of the next trick. The same leader leads again when a trick must be so held aside. If the last trick of the deal is canceled out, the cards are dead and are not scored.

The most convenient way of scoring is to provide a common pool of poker chips or matchsticks. Each player must take from the pool one chip for each point taken (each heart 1, the ♠ Q 13). When a session ends, each player settles with every other as in Black Lady. If the pool nears exhaustion, all players return an equal number of chips to it.

Omnibus Hearts

This latest and best variant of Hearts is Black Lady plus two rules:

The ♦ 10 (in many circles, the ♦ J) counts "plus 10" to whomever takes it in a trick.

If a player wins all thirteen hearts, the ♠ Q and the ♦ 10, he scores plus 26 (in some circles, 36) instead of minus 16.

STRATEGY. The strategy of Black Lady largely applies here. If you could go through a session of Omnibus Hearts, taking no more than an average of one or two hearts per deal, you would very probably win. But you must expect to be "painted" with 13 or more on some occasions. Winning policy is therefore to try to capture the ♦ 10 or make take-all, whenever chances are good, in order to offset the bad hands.

The ♦ 10 is rarely won by the hand that holds it after the pass. Lacking an exceptional hand, the player to whom the ♦ 10 is dealt therefore passes it if he has any good prospect of catching it. The ♦ 10 usually falls by forced discard in the last tricks. After the ♠ Q has been forced out, high cards and long suits are desirable; the object is now to win tricks rather than to lose tricks. It should be noted that if you can catch the ♦ 10 you should usually go for it regardless of the number of hearts you take in the process, for you *may* emerge with a net plus, and in any event it is worthwhile to keep the ♦ 10 from falling to someone else.

The take-all obviously depends on exceptional top strength. But this alone is not sufficient. Most fatal to take-all intentions are low diamonds and low hearts (except as end cards of long near-solid suits), and the ♦ 10. If you cannot pass all such danger cards, don't aim for take-all. On the other hand, aces are not an absolute necessity (except in hearts if you have more than one or two hearts).

Defensive strategy is greatly influenced by the take-all. A successful take-all campaign costs each opponent about

9 points at least. If necessary to prevent a take-all, a player will profit considerably by taking a heart trick (4 points) that he could have lost. He should seldom take or risk taking 7 or 8 points to prevent a take-all unless he is sure it could not be prevented otherwise.

Partnership Hearts

In these variants, four players play in partnerships, either fixed at the beginning of the game or determined during play of each hand.

I. Four players play in partnerships, partners facing each other at the table. Each partnership keeps its tricks together and keep score together. All other rules and variants of Hearts may apply.

II. Four players play in partnerships, partners facing each other at the table. Each player keeps his individual score, and a player must "shoot the moon" alone to earn the bonus points. When an individual's score reaches 100 or more, the scores of the partners are totaled and the partnership with the fewer points wins.

III. Four players play for themselves. At the start of each round, after the deal, there is a bidding round in which each player in order has the opportunity to bid to shoot the moon (take all the tricks). If a player so bids, the bidding round ends and play begins as in Omnibus Hearts. The player holding the ♦ 10 is the unspoken partner of the bidder, and the two players will both receive the same bonus or penalty points for the hand. This silent partner is only revealed to the other players when the ♦ 10 is played. If no one bids to shoot the moon, the hand continues as in normal Omnibus Hearts, each player playing for himself.

POKER

POKER *is a popular game throughout the world. It combines principles of card games known hundreds of years ago in Europe and probably long before that in the Orient, but in its present form it is distinctly of American origin. There are hundreds of forms of Poker, but they differ only in details and all follow the same basic principles, so a person who has learned these principles can play without difficulty in any game. The main divisions of Poker are:* CLOSED POKER, *in which all of a player's cards are unknown to his opponents; and* OPEN POKER, *or* STUD POKER, *in which some of a player's cards are face up and others face down. Closed Poker is now usually encountered in the form of* DRAW POKER. *Subdivisions of these basic forms are:* LOW POKER, *or* LOWBALL, *in which the worst hand wins;* HIGH-LOW POKER, *in which the best and worst hands split; and Freak or Dealer's Choice games. These forms are described separately on the following pages.*

PLAYERS. Two to ten; best for five to eight. More than eight can play only Stud Poker. In all forms of Poker, each plays for himself.

CARDS. A regular pack of 52, occasionally with the addition of the joker. The cards rank: A (high), K, Q, J, 10, 9, 8, 7, 6, 5, 4, 3, 2. The ace also ranks low in the sequence

41

5-4-3-2-A. The joker, when used, is a wild card (see below). Suits are ignored.

Poker is almost invariably played with poker chips of various colors, each color having a different value.

THE DEAL. In every form of Poker the cards are dealt one at a time, in clockwise rotation, beginning with the player at the dealer's left. Usually each player receives five cards, but in various forms of the game more cards are dealt, and often some are dealt face up and some face down. These will be described under the separate forms of Poker.

The first dealer is determined when one player takes a pack of cards and deals it around, face up, until a jack falls to one player, who becomes the first dealer. Thereafter the deal rotates from player to player to the left.

THE PLAY. Poker is a game of betting as to which player holds the best hand. All bets made by all players go in a pile of chips called the *pot,* in the center of the table. The object of the game is to win the pot. The pot may be won in either of two ways: (a) After all players have had full opportunity to bet, there is a *showdown* in which the hands are shown and the best hand wins. (b) If a player makes a bet that no other player is willing to meet, that player wins the pot without showing his hand; for no one may compete for a pot unless he is willing to meet the highest bet made by any other player. This introduces the factor of *bluffing,* betting on a weak hand in the hope that all other players will drop out.

RANK OF POKER HANDS

The following combinations of cards have value in every form of Poker. They are listed in order from highest to lowest.

1. STRAIGHT FLUSH—five cards in sequence in the same suit. As between two straight flushes, the one headed by the highest-ranking card wins: A-K-Q-J-10 (called a *royal flush*) beats K-Q-J-10-9, and 6-5-4-3-2 beats 5-4-3-2-A. The royal flush is the highest standard hand, but when wild cards are used "five of a kind" is the highest.

2. FOUR OF A KIND—any four cards of the same rank. As

between two such hands, the four higher cards win. Four of a kind beats a full house or any lower hand.

3. FULL HOUSE—three of a kind and a pair. As between two full houses, the one wins whose three of a kind are composed of the higher-ranking cards. A full house beats a flush or any lower hand.

4. A FLUSH—any hand of five cards all of the same suit. As between two flushes, the one containing the highest-ranking card wins. If these two cards tie, the next-highest-ranking card decides; if these two cards tie, the third-highest-ranking card, and so on down to the last card, so that ♠A-Q-10-9-3 beats ♥A-Q-10-3-2. A flush beats a straight or any lower hand.

5. A STRAIGHT—any five cards in sequence but not all of the same suit. As between two straights, the one with the highest-ranking card at the head of the sequence is the winner, the highest possible straight being A-K-Q-J-10 and the lowest possible straight being 5-4-3-2-A. A straight beats three of a kind or anything lower.

6. THREE OF A KIND—such as three sixes, with two unmatched cards. If two players each hold three of a kind, the higher-ranking three of a kind wins. This hand beats two pairs or anything lower.

7. TWO PAIRS—two cards of any one rank and two cards of any other rank, with an unmatched card. As between two such hands, the one containing the highest-ranking pair is the winner; if these pairs are the same, the hand with the higher of the two other pairs is the winner; if the two hands contain the identical two pairs, then the higher-ranking unmatched card determines the winner. Two pairs beat any hand with only one pair or with no pair.

8. ONE PAIR—any two cards of the same rank. A pair is dealt to a player about twice in every five hands he holds. As between two hands that have one pair each, the pair composed of the higher-ranking cards wins. If both hands have the same pair, the highest of the three unmatched cards determines the winner; if they are the same, the next highest; and if they are the same, the higher as between the third unmatched cards in the two hands. A hand with only one pair beats any hand which contains no pair and

no one of the combinations described in the preceding paragraphs.

9. HIGH CARD—About one out of two hands that a Poker player holds will consist merely of five unmatched cards. As between two hands of this nature, rank is decided by the rank of the highest card, and if necessary by the next highest, and so on, as described in paragraph 4 above.

OPTIONAL HAND. A *four-flush* is a hand with any four cards of the same suit. In Stud Poker, it is occasionally ruled that a four-flush beats a pair, though it loses to two pairs. In Draw Poker, it is often ruled that a player may open on a four-flush, but if he does not improve it, it is simply ranked as a hand with no pair.

Hands identical in all respects tie; the suits of which the hands are composed never make any difference.

HIGH-LOW POKER. Almost any form of Poker may be played "high-low." There is no difference in the original deal and betting, but in the showdown the highest-ranking poker hand and the lowest-ranking poker hand divide the pot equally. If it cannot be divided equally, the high hand receives any odd chip that is left over. Players must decide in advance whether the ace will rank only high, or either high or low at each player's option.

WILD CARDS. A joker added to a pack or any rank or group of cards (usually deuces), may be designated in advance to be *wild*. The holder of a wild card may cause it to stand for any other card he wishes. Except by special house rules: (a) A wild card ranks exactly the same as the natural card it replaces; and (b) a wild card cannot stand for a card the player already holds, so that there cannot be, for example, a "double-ace-high" flush.

The bug is the joker given restricted wild-card use: It may represent an ace, and it may be used to fill a straight flush, flush, or straight. Therefore two aces and the bug are three aces, but two kings and the bug are merely a pair of kings with an ace.

When wild cards are used, five of a kind are the highest-ranking hand. Ties become possible between identical fours of a kind, full houses, or threes of a kind. In such cases the rank of the other cards in the hand determines the winner.

ROTATION. In Poker the turn to do everything passes

from player to player to the left. The cards are dealt in this way; the turn to bet goes from player to player in rotation. No player should do anything until the player on his right has acted.

RULES OF BETTING

Betting is done during periods of the game called *betting intervals*. The number of betting intervals depends on what form of the game is being played; for example, in Draw Poker the first betting interval occurs when each player has been dealt his full five cards, and in Stud Poker it occurs when each player has been dealt two cards.

In each betting interval, some player has the first right or duty to bet. Usually there is some minimum and some maximum amount, agreed upon in advance, that he may bet. The proper way is for him to place in the pot the number of chips he bets and at the same time announce the number of chips he is betting. When the designated player has bet, each player in turn after him must do one of the following three things:

1. DROP out of the pot (also known as *passing*), which means that he discards his hand and may no longer win the pot. A player may thus drop at any time, and when he drops, all chips he may have put into the pot previously are forfeited to the pot and will eventually go to the winner of it.

2. CALL, which means that he puts in exactly enough chips to make his total contribution to the pot precisely the same as the greatest number of chips put into the pot by any other player. This is also known as *staying in*.

3. RAISE, which means that in addition to enough chips to call he puts in an added amount and now has put in more chips than any other player. The excess is the amount by which he raises, and every other player must either put in as many chips as he, or must drop and forfeit the pot.

For example, a player opens the pot by betting three chips. The next player may call by putting in three chips; he may raise by putting in more than three chips. If he puts in four chips, he has raised one chip; if he puts in six chips, he has raised three chips, and so on. He may not raise by more chips than the limit established for the game.

If the second player does raise three chips, and all the other players drop, the player who opened may stay in by putting three more chips in the pot, for then he will have put in precisely as many chips as the second player.

Betting of this nature continues until all the bets are equalized. The bets are equalized when the turn comes around to the player who in his turn made a higher bet than anyone previous to him, and when every intervening player has either exactly called that bet or dropped.

In many forms of Poker, a player is permitted to *check* if no player before him has opened. Originally this meant that he made the minimum bet, a chip of such low value that it was hardly worthwhile putting it in the pot. So when a player checks, it means he has made "a bet of nothing" and each player in turn after him may also check—in effect calling the bet—until any player makes a genuine bet. Thereafter, each player in turn must call, raise, or drop.

For example, assume a seven-hand game and call the players "A," "B," "C," "D," "E," "F," and "G." "G" is the dealer, so "A" is the eldest hand. Following the deal, "A" and "B" check. "C" opens for five chips (that is, he bets five chips). "D" raises five chips (that is, he puts in ten chips, five to call and five to raise). "E" drops. "F" stays in, putting in ten chips to call. "G" raises ten chips, meaning that he puts in twenty chips in all. "A," who checked on the first round, now has the right to enter the betting, but he drops. "B," who has the same right, puts in twenty chips and calls. "C" calls, putting in fifteen chips (since he put in five chips previously, then fifteen make his total contribution twenty chips, the greatest amount put in by any other player). "D" raises ten more chips, putting in twenty; now he has put in thirty chips altogether. "E," who dropped previously, has no option; once a player drops, he is inactive from that time on. "F," who put in ten chips before, could call by putting in twenty more; but instead he drops, forfeiting the ten chips he put in before. "G" puts in ten chips, making his own total contribution thirty chips, and thus calling the bet. "B" and "C" each put in ten chips, and as in the case of "G" this makes their total contribution the same as any previous player's and means that they both call the previous bet.

Now, of the seven players, three have dropped and the other four have each put in thirty chips, and the turn has come around to "D" again. The bets have been equalized, and "D" may not bet again. This "betting interval" is ended.

Any player who drops out becomes *inactive*; from that time on, the turn to act still passes in rotation from one player to the other, but only from active player to active player.

LIMITS

Most Poker games are played with a limit of anywhere from five to ten chips. Other popular forms of determining a limit are:

Pot Limit. The player making the first bet in any betting interval may bet as many chips as there are in the pot at the time. Any player after him in the same betting interval may raise by as many chips as there are in the pot after he calls. That is, he may announce his intention to raise by "the size of the pot"; then put in enough chips to call the previous bet; then count the pot and match it for a raise.

When playing with a pot limit, some maximum should nevertheless be set for the highest possible bet or raise. Otherwise, in a seven-hand game, this might happen: The antes make 7 chips. The opener opens for 7. The next player puts in 7 to call; now there are 21 chips in the pot, and he raises 21. The third player must put in 28 chips to call, and may now raise 70 chips. This means that the fourth player would have to put up 98 chips merely to call, and could then, if he wished, raise 238.

Table Stakes. A more popular way of playing with a variable limit is to let each player's limit be the number of chips he has at the time. For example, players "A," "B," and "C" are competing for the pot; "A" has a stack of 160 chips, "B" has 110 chips, "C" has only 40. "C" can call any bet made by "A" or "B" for his 40 chips; "B" can call any bet made by "A" for his 110 chips. "A" therefore has 50 chips which he cannot use in this pot.

Suppose "B" bets 70 chips. "C" calls it for 40, that being his limit. "A" calls the entire bet, but does not raise. In the showdown the highest hand takes the main pot, but the side pot—the extra 30 chips each put up by "B" and "A"—go to whichever of them has the higher hand.

When playing with table stakes, no one may add to the chips he has on the table after the deal begins, but between deals he may add as much as he wishes. No one may reduce the number of chips he has on the table until he leaves the game, unless the banker's supply of chips is exhausted and he must buy chips to supply other players.

ARRANGING THE GAME

In addition to the table and chairs necessary to seat all the players comfortably (specially built Poker tables are circular, usually felt-covered, and have pits for holding the players' chips), and at least one pack of playing cards, the only essential equipment for the game is a set of poker chips. The poker chips should be in at least three colors: white, red, and blue. There should be enough of these chips for every player to have an ample supply.

One member of the game is selected as the banker. He may be the host or a player chosen by lot. At the start, all the chips are the banker's property. He sells or issues them to the players, the same initial amount to each player, and keeps a record of the number of chips each player has taken. The white chip is always the basic unit; each red chip is worth five whites, and each blue is worth ten whites. When in the course of a game a player runs out of chips, he should replenish his supply by purchasing an additional "stack" from the banker; he should not borrow or buy from other players. Each stack purchased should be precisely of the same amount as the original issue. If the banker's supply needs replenishment, he should redeem one or more stacks from players who by their winnings have an excess.

At the start of the game, any player picks up the cards, shuffles them, and deals them out face up to the players, one by one, in rotation, until any player gets a jack. That player is the first dealer.

Except that the banker is given first choice of seats, usually no one in a Poker game cares where he sits. Each takes the seat nearest him. If there is any disagreement, the banker shuffles a pack and deals one card to each player, face up; of these cards, the highest-ranking sits at the dealer's left, next highest at his left, and so on. In the course of a game a player may demand a reseating at any time, except that there may not be more than one reseating per hour.

The exact procedure in the game then depends upon which form of Poker has been selected. Most popular is Draw Poker, and that will be described first.

DRAW POKER

In Draw Poker each player is dealt five cards, face down. The undealt cards are set aside for later use and there is a betting interval. Then each active player in turn may discard one or more cards, if he so wishes, and the dealer gives him replacement cards from the top of the pack. There is another betting interval, followed by a showdown in which the highest hand among the active players wins the pot.

In the first betting interval, the eldest hand (player at dealer's left) has the first turn to bet. He may either check or bet; and if he checks, each player after him has the same options, until any player *opens* by making the first bet. Thereafter each player in turn must call, raise, or drop, until the betting interval is over.

In the most popular form of Draw Poker, called JACK-POTS, a player may not open unless he has a pair of jacks or any better hand. In another popular form, called PASS AND OUT (see below), a player may open on anything but in each turn must either bet or drop; there is no checking.

In these forms of Draw Poker, it is customary for each player to ante one white chip (chip of lowest value) before the deal. If no one opens, everyone antes again (the chips from the previous ante remaining in the pot) and there is a new deal by the next dealer in turn.

The draw begins when the bets have been equalized. The dealer picks up the cards left over from the original deal. The first active player to his left may discard one or more cards, naming the number he discards, and the dealer gives him that number of cards from the top of the pack. If a player does not wish to discard and draw, he knocks on the table or otherwise signifies that he is "standing pat." When the first active player to the dealer's left has exercised his right to draw, the next active player in turn to the left discards and draws, and so on until the dealer (or, if he has dropped, the active player nearest his right) has drawn. Now another betting interval begins.

The player who opened has the first turn to bet. He may either bet or check. If he checks, the next active player to his left has the same options. If the opener has dropped, the first active player to his left has the first turn to bet. Once a bet is made, each active player in turn thereafter must either drop, or call, or raise, until the bets are again equalized. When the bets are equalized (or when every player has checked), the second betting interval is ended.

The showdown follows the second betting interval. Every player who has not previously dropped must place all five of his cards face up on the table. It is helpful if each player announces the value of his hand as he does so, as by saying "Three sixes," or "Kings up" (meaning two pairs, the higher of which is a pair of kings), but such announcement is not required. If a player does announce his hand and has more or less than the values he announces, he need not stick by his announcement. It is a tradition of Poker that "the cards speak for themselves." A player may announce three of a kind when in fact he has a full house, and at any time before the pot is actually gathered in by another player he may correct his announcement. A player may not throw away his hand without showing it simply because a previous player has announced a higher-ranking hand; every player who is "in on the call" must expose his full hand face up on the table in the showdown.

When the hands are shown in the showdown, the player showing the highest-ranking poker hand takes in the pot, all the cards are assembled and reshuffled, the players ante for the next pot, and there is another deal by the next dealer in rotation.

OPTIONAL HANDS

In some Draw Poker games, hands other than the standard ones are counted in the showdown. What combinations of cards are so counted depends upon the locality in which the game is played and the preferences of the players. The most popular are listed here:

A *big tiger* is a hand in which the king is the highest card, the eight is the lowest card, and there is no pair; a *little tiger* is a hand in which the eight is the highest card, a three the lowest card, and there is no pair; a *big dog* is a hand in which an ace is the highest card, a nine is the lowest card, and there is no pair; and a *little dog* is a hand in which a seven is the highest card, a deuce is the lowest card, and there is no pair. A big tiger bests a little tiger; either tiger beats a dog; and a big dog beats a little dog. All these hands beat a straight but lose to a flush. (See also *Optional Hand*, page 44.)

When it is necessary to break a tie as between big tigers, little tigers, big dogs, or little dogs, the rules are the same as for breaking ties between any two hands which contain no pair or better.

Lowball

This is Draw Poker except that there are no minimum requirements for opening the pot and in the showdown the lowest-ranking poker hand, instead of the highest, wins the pot.

In Lowball, the ace ranks low only, never high. Straights and flushes do not count. The "bicycle"— 5-4-3-2-A—is the lowest possible hand, whether it is composed all of one suit or of two or more suits. Since aces are low, a pair of aces ranks lower than a pair of deuces.

Very often Lowball is played in connection with regular Draw Poker. If a deal of Draw Poker is passed out, eldest hand picks up the turn again and Lowball is played. A player may check if he wishes, but if no one bets there is still a showdown after the dealer has spoken the second time, and the lowest-ranking hand takes the antes. This game is sometimes called JACKS BACK.

Other Forms of Draw Poker

BLIND AND STRADDLE, also called BLIND OPENING, BLIND TIGER, TIGER (and by other names, including ENGLISH

POKER, AUSTRALIAN POKER, and SOUTH AFRICAN POKER), is a relatively early form of Draw Poker and is still much played.

There is no ante by each player, though the first bet, which will be called the "blind" here, is often called the ante, and in many games the dealer antes one chip, which does not count as a bet. Before the deal, eldest hand must put up one chip as a blind bet; the player at his left must put up two chips as a blind *straddle*; and each player in turn thereafter may, but need not, double the last previous blind bet as an additional straddle. Usually a limit is placed on straddles, so that there may be no more than three straddles, and the largest blind bet before the deal is eight chips.

Five cards are then dealt to each player, and the players look at their hands. The player to the left of the last straddler must either place a voluntary bet of double the amount of the last straddle or must drop out; there is no checking, and no player is permitted to stay in the pot without betting, or calling if there has been a bet previously. When the turn comes around to the ante (eldest hand) again, he may count the amount of his blind opening in figuring how many chips he need put in to call or raise; the same is true of the obligatory straddler and any voluntary straddler.

When all bets have been equalized, there is a draw, and then the active player nearest the left of the dealer must make the first bet in the second betting interval (or, of course, may drop). When the bets are equalized in this betting interval, there is a showdown.

STRAIGHT DRAW POKER is the game described above as PASS AND OUT. It is also called PASSOUT, BET OR DROP, and by other names. Each player in turn, in both the first and second betting intervals, must make a bet (anywhere from the minimum of one white chip up to the limit) or must drop. A player need not have a pair of jacks or better to make a bet of more than one white chip. (In some places, checking is permitted in the second betting interval but not in the first.) This was the earliest form of Draw Poker.

STUD POKER

Five-Card Stud

Stud Poker is the principal form of Open Poker, in which each player has some of his cards face up. The basic form of Stud Poker is now called FIVE-CARD STUD to distinguish it from SEVEN-CARD STUD (described below), which has become at least as popular.

In Five-Card Stud, the dealer gives each player a face-down card, called the *hole card*, and then a face-up card. Each player looks at the face of his hole card but does not show it. Here the deal is interrupted for a betting interval; but from this point on, all cards are dealt face up.

In the first betting interval, the player who was dealt the highest-ranking face-up card must make a bet (if there is a tie for highest-ranking face-up card, the player who first received his card must bet first). After the high-card bets, the betting interval continues until the bets are equalized. A player may drop out at any time, as in any other form of Poker.

The dealer picks up the remainder of the pack and gives each active player another face-up card, and there is another betting interval, commencing again with the player who has the highest poker combination showing. A pair, of course, outranks any combination that does not include a pair; and of two pairs, the higher one outranks the other. If there is no pair, the high card showing determines precedence, and if there is a tie for high card, the second card controls the order, with final determination left to proximity in rotation to the dealer, as in the case of the first card. However, checking is allowed after the first round, and there need be no betting if all active players check.

In the same manner, a third round of face-up cards is dealt to each active player, there is a betting interval, and a final round of face-up cards is dealt to each active player, so that eventually each player has five cards. After a final betting interval, each player who has not dropped turns up his hole card for the showdown.

A player who drops must "fold his hand" by turning

down all his face-up cards. It is poor etiquette for a player who drops to reveal his hole card.

When Five-Card Stud is played high-low, many games allow a player to turn up his hole card before the last card is dealt and receive his last card face down.

OPTIONAL HAND. See page 44.

Seven-Card Stud

Each player receives two cards face down and one card face up, and there is a betting interval. On each subsequent round of dealing, each active player receives a face-up card until he has four face-up cards (and, of course, two face-down cards) with a betting interval following the dealing of each face-up card all around. Finally a third face-down card is dealt to each player, there is a final betting interval, and each player who has at least called the final bet turns his three hole cards face up, selects any five of his cards to be a poker hand, and there is a showdown.

This game is often called DOWN-THE-RIVER, SEVEN-TOED PETE, and by other names.

SIX-CARD STUD POKER (which is identical with Five-Card Stud Poker except that after the fourth face-up card and the fourth betting interval each player receives a second face-down card, followed by a final betting interval) and EIGHT-CARD STUD POKER (which is the same as Seven-Card Stud except that after the seventh card is dealt and there is a betting interval, an eighth card is dealt face down to each active player and there is a final betting interval) are also played, but not so often. In each case, the player selects five of his cards to represent his poker hand in the showdown.

Seven-Card High-Low Stud

A player may select any of his cards to compete for the high end of the pot and a different five cards to compete for the low end, and therefore may win both ways. (Note that in high-low, a perfect low is 6-4-3-2-A.) Often *declarations* are played: After the final round of betting is finished but before the showdown, each player declares whether he is trying for high, for low, or for both. He may win only the part of the pot for which he declares. If a player declares for both high and low he must at least tie each way or he receives nothing.

There are two popular forms of declaration. In *simultaneous declaration*, each player conceals a chip (or some other token) in his closed fist. Different chips (or tokens) are used to indicate the three different calls—high, low, and high-low. All reveal the declarations simultaneously. In *consecutive declaration,* one player is designated as the first to declare, usually the player who made the last aggressive move (raise or bet) on the final betting round (or the high hand, if there was no bet on the final round). Declaration then proceeds in clockwise rotation. The former method is preferable, because it eliminates the advantage of position which plays a large role in the second.

DEALER'S CHOICE

Most Poker games played casually by friendly social groups are "Dealer's Choice" games, under the following rules:

1. Each dealer, as his turn comes, may state the game which will be played—Draw Poker, Stud Poker, or any form of either game.

2. If any card is to be wild, the dealer may designate that card or cards.

3. The next dealer is not bound by the previous dealer's choice. If a selected game is one which may be passed out, in the case of a passed-out hand the same dealer deals again.

4. A dealer is not limited to the most common forms of Poker, those that have previously been described in these pages. He may select any of the games described in the following pages, or any game of his invention or knowledge which is simple enough to be described and understandable to the other players without too great a loss of time.

Spit in the Ocean

Each player antes. After each player has received four face-down cards, as in Draw Poker, the dealer places one card from the top of the pack face up in the center of the table. This card is wild, and all other cards of the same rank are wild. Each player may use this card as part of his hand. There is a betting interval, followed by a showdown.

VARIATION 1. Instead of one card, the dealer places three cards face up in the center, and each player may select any one of these cards to be the fifth card in his hand and to be wild, together with every other card of the same rank in his hand.

VARIATION 2. The dealer places only one card in the center, but after the betting interval each player turns up any one card from his hand and there is another betting interval; then a second card and a betting interval; and so on, until when each player turns up his last face-down card there is a showdown.

Cincinnati

After giving each player five cards as in Draw Poker, the dealer places five cards face down in the center of the table. There is a betting interval as in Draw Poker.

The dealer then turns up one of the center cards, and there is another betting interval; then the second, third, fourth, and fifth of these cards, with a betting interval after each.

After the last betting interval there is a showdown in which each player selects any five cards from among the cards dealt to him and the cards on the table to be his poker hand.

Criss-Cross

This game is no different from Cincinnati except that the center cards are laid out in the shape of a cross. The card in the center of the cross is turned up last. This card is wild, and so is any other card of the same rank. Each player must select his poker hand from among his own five cards plus either row of three cards in the cross.

Lamebrain Pete

This game is the same as Cincinnati, except that the lowest exposed card and all other cards of the same rank are wild.

Omaha

The same as Cincinnati, except that each player is dealt two cards instead of five. After the last betting interval he selects any five cards, from among the five cards in the center and the two dealt to him, to be his hand.

Shotgun

The deal and draw are as in Draw Poker, except as follows: After each player has received three cards, the deal is suspended for a betting interval. Each player receives another face-down card, and there is another betting interval. Each player receives a fifth face-down card, and there is another betting interval. Then there is a draw, as in Draw Poker, followed by a final betting interval. At the end of the final betting interval, the players still in the pot show their hands.

Texas Hold'em

Two cards are dealt face down to each player, followed by a betting round. The first two players to the left of dealer must make *blind* bets—without looking at their cards—which function like an ante. On the first round, players may either call or raise the blind bet, or they must fold their hand (there is no checking). After the first round of betting, three common cards, called the *flop*, are dealt face-up in the center of the table. There is another round of betting. On this and each succeeding round, players may check if no one has bet when it is their turn to bet. Then a fourth common card, called the *turn*, is exposed and there is another round of betting. Then the last common card, known as the *river*, is turned up followed by the last round of betting. The winning hand is the best five-card poker hand using any combination of the player's two cards and the five common cards.

Pineapple

Three cards are dealt face down to each player. There is a betting round. Then three common cards are dealt face up in the center of the table. There is another betting round. Each player must then discard one of his cards. A fourth common card is then dealt face up in the center followed by another betting round, and finally a fifth common card is dealt followed by a final betting round. Each player chooses the best five cards from among the two in his hand and the common cards. The game can be played either high or high-low.

Seven Twenty-Seven

In this game, a combination of BLACKJACK and HIGH-LOW POKER, players try to make a hand whose points total as near as possible to 7 or 27 points (hence the name!). To this purpose, cards are counted as follows: Aces = 1 or 11 points, face cards = ½ point, all other cards = face value. The same ace may be counted as 1 point for the purpose of making 7 and as 11 for the purpose of making 27. Each player antes and then dealer gives each player one card face up and one card face down. The players look at their face-down card and in turn may ask for an additional face-down card. There is then a betting round, as in Poker. After each round of betting, the remaining players can each ask for an extra face-down card or keep their hand as it is. A player can pass a chance to take a card on one round and then take a card on the next. If no one wants an extra card there is a showdown. The winners are the player whose total is nearest to seven and the player whose total is nearest to twenty-seven.

Three-Card Poker or Three-Card Monte

Each player receives three cards, all dealt face down, but the deal is interrupted after each round for a betting interval. After the dealing of the third card and the third betting interval, there is a showdown in which three of a kind is the highest hand; then come a three-card straight flush; a three-card flush; a three-card straight; a pair; and high card as among three otherwise unmatched cards.

This game is also played high-low, with the ace ranking high in a high hand and low in a low hand. Usually declarations are required (see page 54).

Two-Card Poker

Each player receives two cards, face down. There is one betting interval and a showdown. Straights and flushes do not count, a pair being the highest hand and high cards determining the rank as among hands with no pair.

This game is usually played with wild cards, either deuces or "one-eyes" (the jacks of spades and hearts, and the king of diamonds). It is often played high-low, with the ace ranking high in the high hand and low in the low hand. Usually declarations are required (see page 54).

Hurricane

Two-card poker played at high-low (often with deuces wild).

Red and Black

In betting and settlement, Red and Black is the same as High-Low Poker, but it is not the rank of poker hands which decides the result. All red cards have a "plus" value and all black cards a "minus" value. Aces count 1 each, face cards 10 each, other cards as many points as the numbers showing on their faces. If a player has ♥ K Q ♦ 7 ♠ 9 ♣ 4 he is "plus 14," because he has 27 points in plus cards and 13 points in minus cards.

There is a deal of five cards and a betting interval as in Draw Poker; then a draw and another betting interval, followed by a showdown in which the highest hand and the lowest hand divide the pot. Theoretically, of course, the "highest" hand can be the lowest minus, or the "lowest" hand can be the smallest plus.

Mexican Stud

There is no difference between this game and Five-Card Stud Poker (pages 53-54) except that all cards are dealt face down. After each card is dealt, each player may turn up one of his cards and leave any card he pleases face down as his hole card.

Baseball

Seven-Card Stud is played, with all ninespots wild and with any three in the hole wild, and with these special rules:

1. The first player who is dealt a threespot face up must decide either to drop out of the pot or to "buy the pot" (pay a forfeit to the pot equivalent to the number of chips already in the pot) and stay in. If he does buy the pot, from that time onward all threes are wild whether in the hole or not.

2. If a player is dealt a four, face up, he may either keep it or discard it and have it replaced by another card. A four dealt face down has no special significance.

In either case, a player must make his decision (and make the required contribution, if any, to the pot) before another card is dealt. A card dealt in the meantime is dead.

Football

The same as Baseball, except that all sixes and fours are wild, a four dealt face up requires the player to match the pot or drop, and a deuce dealt face up entitles the player to a free hole card, dealt immediately.

Knock Poker

Best for three to five players. There is an ante from each player, then five cards are dealt face down to each player; the undealt cards are placed in the center of the table to form the stock. The player to dealer's left draws the top card of the stock and discards, and thereafter each player in turn has his choice between the top card of the stock and the top discard. The discard pile should be kept squared up and is not open for inspection.

Any player, in turn, after drawing and before discarding, may *knock*. This means there will be a showdown when his turn comes again. The knocker then discards, and each player has one more turn in which he may draw as usual, and then he must either drop and pay the knocker a chip or discard and stay in.

When knocker's turn comes again, he does not draw—there is a showdown among all the players who stayed in. If the knocker has the high hand, every player who stayed in pays him two chips. If any other player ties the knocker, they divide the winnings, except that the knocker keeps chips paid to him by players who dropped out. If anyone beats the knocker, he gets the antes, and the knocker pays two chips to every player who stayed in.

It is customary for bonuses to be paid (by every player, including those who may have dropped) as follows: two chips each for knocking on the first round and winning without drawing a card; one chip each for knocking before drawing on the first round, then drawing the top card of the stock and winning; four chips each for winning with a royal flush, two chips each for winning with any other straight flush, and one chip each for winning with four of a kind.

Butcher Boy

All cards are dealt face up. When any player receives a card which is of the same rank as a card previously dealt, it is transferred to the hand of the player who received the card of that rank previously. There is a betting interval, with the player to whom the card was transferred having the first right to bet. When the betting interval is ended, the deal continues, the first card going to the player who would have received the last card.

Butcher Boy is usually played with high and low splitting the pot. There is no decision until any player has four of a kind, whereupon he takes half the pot. The other half goes to the low hand. Since not all players have exactly five cards, low hand is determined as follows: A player with more than five cards may select any five to be his low hand. A player with fewer than five cards is deemed to have the lowest card in the pack to make up each gap; for example, a three-card hand 8-5-4 is treated as 8-5-4-double 2 (not a pair of deuces) and beats a natural 8-5-4-3-2 for low.

Anaconda

Each player is dealt seven cards, face down. There is a round of betting (sometimes omitted), after which each player still in the pot passes three cards to his left (or right, as agreed). Each player then discards two cards, leaving himself five cards for his final hand. After a round of betting, each remaining player stacks his five cards in the order in which he intends to expose them. (This order may not be changed during the course of the hand.) After each player has determined his order, each turns a card. There is another round of betting. Each player then flips (turns over) a second card and there is another round of betting, and so on, until a showdown is reached.

Put and Take

This is often played in Dealer's Choice Poker games, though some bar it because the dealer has a great advantage.

Each player antes one chip. The first dealer is selected by lot, and thereafter the deal rotates. The dealer takes no cards, but gives each player except himself five face-up cards, dealt one at a time.

The dealer then turns up five "put" cards, one at a time. As each card is turned up, any player whose hand contains a card of the same rank must put into the pot a certain number of chips: one chip if it is the first card turned up, two if it is the second, four if it is the third, eight if it is the fourth, and sixteen if it is the fifth. A player having two or more cards of the rank in his hand must put up for each.

The dealer then turns up five "take" cards, and for each card a player having a card of the same rank in his hand takes from the pot one chip on the first card, two on the second, four on the third, eight on the fourth, and sixteen on the fifth. Again, if he has two or more cards of the same rank in his hand, he takes the full number of chips for each.

If there are any chips left in the pot, the dealer takes them. If the pot does not have enough chips to supply what the players are entitled to take, the dealer must make good. The dealer has an advantage because of the original antes.

Indian Poker

One card is dealt face down to each player. Each player, without looking at his card, simultaneously places it on his forehead so each player can see all cards but his own. There is a single round of betting and a showdown. Highest card wins.

IRREGULARITIES IN POKER

SHUFFLE, CUT. Any player may shuffle, but the dealer has the right to do so last. The cards must be shuffled at least three times. The dealer must offer the cards to the player at his right and that player must cut them. No fewer than five nor more than forty-seven cards may be lifted off the pack in cutting.

NEW DEAL. Any player who has not intentionally looked at the face of his first card and who has not received his second card may call for a new deal if the rules of the shuffle and cut were not fully observed. It is a misdeal, the dealer loses his deal and the next player in turn deals, if, at any time before the pot is gathered in, the pack is proved to be incorrect (to have the wrong number of cards, or a duplication of cards); or if more than one card is improperly exposed in dealing and if the misdeal is demanded by a player who receives such an improperly exposed card and who has not intentionally looked at the face of any other card dealt to him; or if more than two players receive an incorrect number of cards.

INCORRECT HAND. If two players have incorrect hands, one having a card too many and another having a card too few, the dealer may correct it by drawing from the hand with too many cards and giving the excess to the hand with too few. If only one player has an incorrect number of cards, and announces the fact before he looks at any of them, the dealer must correct his hand by drawing the excess from a hand with too many cards and restoring it to the top of the pack; or by supplying a short hand with a card or cards from the top of the pack.

However, a player who has too many cards and has intentionally looked at any of them has a dead hand and must drop out. The player who has too few cards and has intentionally looked at any of them may play on, but must play throughout with a short hand and cannot make a straight, flush, or straight flush.

CARD EXPOSED IN DEALING. Cards exposed prior to the betting interval are dealt with under the paragraph "New Deal" above.

In Draw Poker, if a card is exposed in the draw, the player due to receive it must take the first such card but may not take any subsequent exposed card. Such cards exposed in the draw are placed with the discards. The draw is continued until all other players are satisfied. The player whose cards were exposed may then receive cards from the top of the pack to satisfy his requirements; or may require that the remainder of the pack, together with all discards except his own (and the discards of the opener, if they have been kept separate), be shuffled by the dealer, and cut by him, before the remainder of his draw is dealt to him.

In Stud Poker, if the dealer prematurely exposes a card to be dealt for the next round of dealing, that card is placed with the discards. Other players may receive the cards they would have received if no irregularity had occurred, provided this is possible. The players who would have received the cards exposed then receive their cards from the top of the pack.

PLAYER DEALT OUT. If the leader omits a player in dealing, he must give his own hand to that player. If he omits more than one player in dealing, his own hand (if any) goes to the player omitted nearest his left, and no other player has any recourse.

If the dealer improperly gives a player a card face up instead of face down, that player has no immediate recourse but the dealer must give him his next card face down. This remedy may continue without penalty on the part of the dealer, unless it is repeated, until and including the player's fourth face-up card. At that point the player may, if he wishes, withdraw from the pot all chips he has put in and the dealer must pay a penalty to the pot equivalent to the number of chips withdrawn. If the player chooses to play with all his cards face up, and to withdraw no chips from the pot, the dealer is not subject to penalty.

BET OUT OF TURN. No chips once placed in the pot may be removed from the pot except as provided in the preceding paragraph. If a player bets out of turn, his bet is void, his chips remain in the pot, and the player in proper turn may act. When the offender's turn comes, he may use the chips he put in to call the preceding bet, if they are sufficient to that purpose; and he may add to them sufficient chips to call the preceding bet, if necessary; but he may not raise, even if his out-of-turn contribution to the pot was more than is required to call.

DROPPING OUT OF TURN. A player may drop without waiting for his turn if there is only one other player in the pot. If there is any other player in the pot, and he drops out of turn, when his turn comes he must call any bet made by any player before him, but his hand is dead and cannot win the pot.

INCORRECT NUMBER OF CARDS. If a player has too many or too few cards and the error is not corrected as provided above: a player with too few cards may compete for the pot, but cannot make a straight, flush, or straight flush; a hand with too many cards is dead and cannot win the pot.

INCORRECT ANNOUNCEMENT. A player who announces a bet and does not put in enough chips to conform to the announcement must on demand supply enough chips to call, if so many chips were not previously put into the pot, and may not raise; and if he put into the pot enough chips to raise but not enough to conform to his announcement he is deemed to have called and any additional chips are forfeited.

INCORRECT DRAW. A player who is given by dealer the wrong number of cards (any number of cards not conforming to his discards) and who looks at any of them cannot have his draw corrected. If the result gives him too few cards, he may play on. If the result gives him too many cards, his hand is dead. If he has not looked at any of the cards, he may demand a correction by the dealer.

DRAW OUT OF TURN. A player may not draw if he has permitted a player to his left to draw out of turn. He may stand pat on the cards originally dealt to him, unless he has discarded. If he has discarded, his hand is dead.

ERROR IN OPENING. The opener is permitted to split his openers (for example, to discard a queen from Q-Q-J-10-9 and draw one card to a straight) without announcing the fact. He may place his discard in the pot so that it cannot be shuffled up with other discards and so that he can reclaim it to prove that he had openers.

If the opener cannot prove to the satisfaction of other players that he held openers, his hand is dead and cannot win the pot. Any chips he has placed in the pot are forfeited. If no one has called his bet, the antes plus his opening bet remain in the pot for the next deal. If his bet has been called, his own hand is dead but play continues.

The opener's hand is dead if he has more than five cards, and the penalty is the same as though he lacked openers. If no one calls his bet, he need show only enough cards face up to prove he had openers, and the remainder of his hand face down to prove that he had no more than five cards.

ETHICS AND ETIQUETTE

Each group of Poker players is likely to set its own standards of ethical behavior, and a stranger in the game is well advised to learn what these standards are, so he will not be thought unsporting.

Old-fashioned Poker players feel that so long as a player does not actually cheat, he should not be bound by any code of ethics. Most players feel, however, that there is a limit beyond which one should not venture in misrepresenting his hand.

One may misrepresent one's hand in a bantering way, as by saying, "Go ahead and call me; you know I'm always bluffing," or words to that effect, when in fact one has a good hand.

It is not unethical to bet on a sure thing, nor is it unethical to check with a strong hand, intending to raise if anyone else bets.

One should not intentionally break the rules of the game, even when willing to pay the penalty.

Partnerships are contrary to the spirit of the game, and even when husband and wife are in the same game they should treat each other as opponents in the play.

It is not unethical to draw one card to four of a kind, even though the draw cannot improve the hand. (And if a player is lucky enough to hold four of a kind, what does he care what the ethics are?)

STRATEGY OF POKER

To become a good player, one must:

1. Learn the poker hands thoroughly.

2. Learn the relative values of the hands—what sort of hand may be expected to win the pot.

3. Learn how many cards it is best to draw to the various poker combinations.

4. Learn the odds against winning with any particular hand, and how to figure the odds offered "by the pot."

5. Observe the other players in the game, to learn their habits and to read their probable strength or weakness from their actions and mannerisms; and at the same time avoid giveaway mannerisms of one's own.

The relative values of the hands depend on how many players are in the game (or how many are in the pot, for if there are seven players in the game but two have dropped, the circumstances are precisely the same as if there were five in the game and none had dropped). The value of the hand depends also upon what betting there has been: A pair of aces may be an excellent holding when all the other players have checked, but is not worth much if two or three players have already raised, for their raises advertise their holding of strong hands.

In general, one should appraise one's hand as follows in a seven-player game:

When one is dealt a straight or any better hand, one will almost always win the pot and it will pay one to bet or raise even if two other players have previously raised.

When one is dealt three of a kind, one will usually win

the pot, and one should raise even if another player has previously raised; but one should only call if two players have previously raised.

When one is dealt two pairs, it is about 2 to 1 that one has the best hand before the draw; but at the same time it is 11 to 1 that one will not improve one's hand in the draw. Especially if the higher of one's two pairs is anything less than queens, one is in danger of losing the pot to another player who will draw three cards to a pair and improve. For this reason, it is wise for a player with two pairs to raise immediately. The raise usually drives out some players who might otherwise stay and improve their hands.

When one is dealt a pair of aces, it is odds-on that no other player has as good a hand. A player holding aces or any better hand should open the pot in any position and should stay in even if the pot has been raised.

A pair of kings has an even chance of being the best hand when only five or six players remain; a pair of queens, when only four players remain. Holding one of these hands, one should open the pot against the stated number of players but should usually drop if the pot is raised. The last three players at the table, after the first four have checked, may safely open the pot on a pair of jacks.

When another player has opened the pot, it must be remembered that he has at least jacks and probably has an even better hand. It is seldom wise to stay in without a pair of queens or better, except (a) when four or five players have stayed in and there is no danger that anyone will raise; or (b) when you have a straight or flush possibility and the pot is large enough to warrant drawing to it.

A four-flush offers nine chances in forty-seven to make a flush. This means that the odds are more than 4 to 1 against you when you draw one card to a four-flush. If there is at least four times as much money in the pot as you have to put in, such a hand is worth playing. If there is anything less in the pot, the hand should be dropped. Likewise with a double-ended straight (any four cards in sequence, except A-K-Q-J or 4-3-2-A): The odds are 5 to 1 against filling it, and the pot must offer at least that much to make playing worthwhile. A combination such as A-K-

Q-J, 4-3-2-A, or 7-6-4-3 ("inside" straight) is almost never worth playing; the odds are 11 to 1 against filling it.

DRAW POKER. When drawing to a pair, discard three cards and hold only the pair. To keep an ace or other high card as a "kicker" seriously decreases the chances of improving. For example, holding

it would be unwise to hold the two nines and the ace and draw only two cards. This maneuver has little value as a bluff—it is unlikely to make anyone think you hold three of a kind, unless you follow through on the bluff all the way by raising heavily before the draw and betting after the draw, and this is a losing game in the long run.

Likewise, when you hold three of a kind it is best in most cases to throw away both the odd cards and draw two. The only exception is when you have raised before the draw and it seems that another player has two high pairs. If you draw two cards, he may refuse to call a bet. If you hold either of your odd cards and draw only one, he may call.

A player who has opened with a hand like this:

or with a pair and a four-flush, like this:

is often tempted to "split his openers" and draw one card to his straight or flush possibility. However, unless there is enough in the pot to offer 4-to-1 or 5-to-1 odds respectively, it is usually better to draw to the pair. The only exception is when the opener has a four-card straight flush possibility, in which case it is advantageous to split the openers and draw one card. The odds are only 2 to 1 against improving if the straight flush is open at both ends, and 3 to 1 if it is open at only one end.

STUD POKER. Since there is no draw to the original five cards, the average winning hand is lower than in Draw Poker. The player decides on his action after seeing all but one card in every other hand, and is in a better position to judge whether or not to play, or to raise.

Usually a player should drop out when his cards, including his hole card, are beaten by the showing cards of any other player. If another player shows a pair, one should not stay in without a higher pair.

With a concealed pair (a pair which includes the hole card), raise immediately. With an open pair, bet the limit immediately. (In both cases, assuming that no other player shows a higher pair.)

It is seldom wise to bet against a player whose hole card may give him a hand you cannot possibly beat.

DEUCES WILD. This is a much maligned game. Most people think of "deuces wild" as the afternoon diversion of silly women who do not even know the rank of the poker hands. Actually, Deuces Wild is at least as scientific a game as regular Draw Poker.

The considerations in the two games are about the same except that two pairs are almost valueless in Deuces Wild. A straight will win more often than not, but is not worth more than one raise.

It is usually advisable to open on any hand containing a deuce; one should also open on a pair of aces. Two low pairs should be opened only by the last two players in turn, after all others have checked; they should be thrown away or split if any other player opens. A sequence of three cards plus a deuce should be played even if the pot is small at the time.

Do not raise before the draw with less than three aces (including at least one deuce), or a pair of deuces.

If your hand contains two deuces, draw three cards to them unless you also have an ace, in which case hold the ace.

ODDS IN POKER

It doesn't help much to know the chances of being dealt a straight flush or a full house or even a pair. But it does help to know the odds against improving any particular hand. The odds for the most frequently encountered situations are given below.

DRAW POKER		ODDS
DRAW	RESULT	AGAINST
Three cards to a Pair	Two pairs	5¼ to 1
	Triplets	7¾ to 1
	Full House	97 to 1
	Four of a Kind	360 to 1
	Any improvement	2½ to 1
Two cards to a Pair & Ace	Aces up	7½ to 1
	Another pair	17 to 1
	Total two pairs	4¾ to 1
	Triplets	12 to 1
	Full House	120 to 1
	Four of a Kind	1,080 to 1
	Aces up or better	4 to 1
	Any improvement	2¾ to 1
Two cards to Triplets	Full House	15⅓ to 1
	Four of a Kind	22½ to 1
	Any improvement	8⅔ to 1
One card to Triplets	Full House	14⅔ to 1
	Four of a Kind	46 to 1
	Any improvement	10¾ to 1
Four to an Ace	Aces or better	3 to 1
	Two pairs or better	11 to 1
	Aces up or better	14 to 1
Three to A-K of same suit	Two pairs or better	12 to 1
Two to a three-straight-flush	Two pairs or better	7½ to 1
(such as J 10 9)	Straight or better	11 to 1

DRAW POKER   ODDS
DRAW   RESULT   AGAINST

(such as Q J 10 or 4 3 2)	Straight or better	13½ to 1
(such as A K Q or 3 2 A)	Straight or better	20 to 1
Two to a Straight (open-end)	Straight	22 to 1
Two to a flush	Flush	23 to 1
One to two pairs	Full House	10¾ to 1
One to a four-flush	Flush	4¼ to 1
One to a straight (open end)	Straight	5 to 1
(inside)	Straight	10¾ to 1
One to a straight-flush		
(open end)	Straight flush	22½ to 1
	Straight or better	2 to 1
(inside)	Straight flush	46 to 1
	Straight or better	3 to 1

STUD POKER

CHANCE OF HAVING THE HIGH HOLE CARD (OUT OF 100)

	No. of Opponents							
Your Hole Card	1	2	3	4	5	6	7	8
Ace	94	89	83	79	74	70	66	62
King	86	74	63	55	47	40	35	30
Queen	78	61	48	37	29	23	18	14
Jack	70	49	34	24	17	12	8	5

FIVE-CARD STUD

ODDS AGAINST EVENTUALLY PAIRING YOUR HOLE CARD

	Odds Against Pairing If Your Hole Card Is	Odds Against Pairing If Your Hole Card Is
No. of Players	*Unmatched on Table*	*Matched Once on Table*
Seven or eight	4 to 1	6 to 1
Five or six	5 to 1	7 to 1

After you have received an unmatched card for your
third card:

No. of Other Players' Cards You Have Seen	Odds Against Pairing If Your Hole Card Has Not Been Matched	Odds Against Pairing If Your Hole Card Has Been Matched
Nine to twelve	5½ to 1	9 to 1
Five to eight	6½ to 1	10 to 1

If you have a pair and an odd card, under normal conditions the odds against improving to better than a high pair are 2½ to 1 if you have seen no card matching either of the ranks you hold, but 3¼ to 1 if a card matching your pair or odd card has appeared. (If two matching cards have appeared, you should almost always drop out, the odds against eventual improvement being prohibitive.)

SEVEN-CARD STUD (HIGH)
ODDS AGAINST MAKING A DESIRED HAND

Desired Hand	*Holding*	*Odds Against*
Full House or better	Three of a kind	1½ to 1
	" plus two odd cards	2 to 1
	" plus three odd cards	4 to 1
	One pair plus one odd card	13 to 1
	One pair plus two odd cards	19 to 1
	One pair plus three odd cards	39 to 1
	Two pairs	4 to 1
	Two pairs plus one odd card	4 to 1
	Two pairs plus two odd cards	10 to 1
Flush	Three of a suit	4½ to 1
	" plus one odd card	9 to 1
	" plus two odd cards	23 to 1
	Four of a suit	1¼ to 1
	" plus one odd card	1¾ to 1
	" plus two odd cards	4¼ to 1
Straight	J 10 9	4¼ to 1
	J 10 9 2	8 to 1
	J 10 9 3 2	20 to 1
	J 10 9 8	1⅓ to 1
	J 10 9 8 2 (or A Q J 10 8)	2¼ to 1
	J 10 9 8 3 2 (or A Q J 10 8 2)	4¾ to 1
	J 10 9 7	2¾ to 1
	J 10 9 7 2	4½ to 1
	J 10 9 7 3 2	10 to 1
	K Q J (or 4 3 2)	6¾ to 1
	K Q J 2 (or K 4 3 2)	12 to 1
	A K Q (or 3 2 A)	13 to 1
	A K Q 2 (or J 3 2 A)	24 to 1

SEVEN-CARD HIGH-LOW STUD
(assuming a straight does not count as low)

Your Hand	Odds Against Making a Seven-Low	Odds Against Making No Worse Than an Eight-Low	Odd Against Making No Worse Than a Nine-Low
7 3 2	4 to 1	4 to 1	Even
7 3 2 K	8 to 1	4 to 1	2 to 1
7 3 2 K Q	24 to 1	10 to 1	6 to 1
7 4 3 2	1½ to 1	2 to 3	1 to 3
7 4 3 2 K	2 to 1	1¼ to 1	2 to 3
7 4 3 2 K Q	5 to 1	3 to 1	2 to 1
*4 3 2	6½ to 1	2¾ to 1	Even
*4 3 2 K	13 to 1	4 to 1	2¼ to 1

---

* If straights do count as low, use figures given for 7 3 2, 7 3 2 K, etc.

SOLITAIRE

SOLITAIRE *or* PATIENCE *games, in their many different forms, probably have a larger following than any other kind of card game. With rare exceptions, a solitaire game is a matter of laying out a "tableau," or original layout; and then, turning up cards from the "stock," or undealt cards, trying to build up piles of cards which match in rank, color, suit, etc. On this basic pattern, however, there are countless possible variants. The ones described here are among the most popular.*

KLONDIKE

KLONDIKE *is probably the most widely known solitaire game. It is frequently called* CANFIELD, *but actually the game played at Canfield's in Saratoga in the gay nineties was quite different (see below). Klondike is also known under a variety of local names, such as* FASCINATION, DEMON PATIENCE, *the* CHINAMAN. Chance of winning: 1 in 30 games.

One regular pack is used. Deal twenty-eight cards into seven piles. The first pile at the left has one card, the second two, and so on up to seven in the last pile. The uppermost card of each pile is face up; all the rest are face down.

The dealing is crosswise, one card to each pile, dealing to one less pile each time, and turning the first card in each round face up.

On the piles you may build in descending sequence, red on black or black on red. For example, on the ♠ K may be placed either ♦ Q or ♥ Q. All the face-up cards on a pile may be moved as a unit, and matched according to the bottom card. For example, if you have built the ♣ 7 on the ♦ 8, you can later move the two together onto the ♠ 9. When you uncover a face-down card on a pile, turn it face up. You are entitled to have seven piles, and if one is entirely removed you may put a king in the space.

Each time you free an ace, move it into a row above the piles. On the aces you may build up in suit and sequence, and to win the game you have to build each up to the king. Once played up on these foundations, a card may not be withdrawn to help elsewhere.

From the rest of the pack, the stock, turn up cards one by one. Put cards that you cannot use at once into one waste pile. You may always play off the top card of the waste pile. You may go through the stock only once.

An example beginning:

The face-up cards in your original layout are

Put the ♠ A in the foundation row and build the ♠ 2 on it. Put the ♣ 7 on the ♥ 8. Turn up the cards uncovered; suppose they are ♣ 9, ♥ K, ♦ 3. Move the pile from the left end (the ♥ 8 at bottom) onto the ♣ 9. That gives you a space, into which you can move either ♥ K or ♠ K.

CANFIELD

CANFIELD *is named after the proprietor of a famous gambling dive at Saratoga. Here one could buy a pack of cards* *for $50 and play a game of Canfield under the watchful eye of the croupier, then receive $5 back for every card in the foundation piles, or $500 if one got all fifty-two cards out. Mathematicians do not attempt to calculate the odds on getting off eleven or more cards, but Mr. Canfield found them right and made a fortune.* Chance of winning: 1 in 30 games.

Shuffle a regular pack and first count off thirteen cards from the top. Place them face up at your left. These cards are the *stock*. The next card of the pack is your first foundation ($5 back already!); put it above and to right of the stock. Then to the right of the stock deal four cards face up, starting your *tableau*.

Whatever the rank of the first foundation, the other three cards of the same rank are also foundations. When (and if!) they become available, put them up beside the first. Build up on the foundations in suit and sequence; the rank in the suit is circular, the ace being above the king and below the deuce. (For example, if the first foundation were the ♣ 10, you, would build with first the ♣ J, then ♣ Q, ♣ K, ♣ A, ♣ 2 and so on up to the ♣ 9.) You win the game if you build each foundation up to thirteen cards.

On the tableau you may build down, red on black and black on red. For example, the ♥ J can go on either the ♣ Q or ♠ Q. One card at a time may be moved from the top of a tableau pile, or all may be moved as a unit. In the latter case, the bottom card must of course match correctly with the top card of the pile on which it is placed. For example, a pile ♣ 8, ♥ 7, ♠ 6 may be moved onto a red 9.

On the layout below, move the ♥ 7 up to the foundation

row beside the ♣ 7. Build the ♣ K on the ♥ A. Fill the two spaces of the tableau from the stock. Then another space can be made by moving the ♥ A and ♣ K onto the ♠ 2.

The thirty-four cards remaining after you have dealt are the *hand*. Turn up cards from the hand in packets of three, placing them in one waste pile, face up. You may play off the top card of the waste pile onto foundations or tableau, thus releasing lower cards one by one. After you have exhausted the hand, pick up the waste pile without shuffling, turn it over, and there is your new hand. You may run through the hand by threes as many times as you wish, until play comes to a standstill.

You are entitled to have four tableau piles. If any pile is cleared away, making a space, fill it with the top card of the stock. After the stock is exhausted, spaces may be filled from the hand. Usually if the game reaches this stage it can be won. The great difficulty is to get all your stock cards into play.

In Mr. Canfield's gambling house, you could turn up the cards one at a time and go through them only once; or turn them up three at a time and go through them only three times. It has been estimated that the average was only five or six cards played.

Pounce

This is Canfield played by two or more players (up to about seven). Each player has his own pack and his own tableau. (Be careful that no two packs have the same back design.) Aces are foundations and are moved to the center when available. They belong to and are played on by all the players. The winner of a game is the first to get rid of his reserve pile. Players should establish rules of procedure to avoid chaos.

ACES UP

Also known as ACES HIGH *or* IDIOT'S DELIGHT. *An easy game to play but difficult to win.* Chance of winning: 1 in 10 games.

There are four tableau piles and a discard pile, all of which start out empty. Deal four cards, face up, one onto each tableau pile. If two or more of those cards have the same suit, move the lower-ranked ones onto the discard pile. When you can make no more moves, deal four more cards onto the tableaus such that the previous cards are visible. Only the topmost card of each tableau is available. Continue to move cards to the discard if they match the suit of any higher-ranked available card. If a pile is emptied, you must fill it with an available card from another tableau before you can deal again. Because aces are high, they cannot be discarded. The goal is to complete the game with all other cards discarded, and the aces laid out, one in each tableau.

BAKER'S DOZEN

Chance of winning: 2 out of 3 games.

Lay out the entire deck in thirteen tableau piles of four cards each, face up and overlapped so that all cards are visible. When a king appears on a pile, move it to the bottom of that pile, so that no lower-ranked cards start out under the kings. Four foundations start the game empty. Top cards of tableaus are available for building on each other, and on the foundations. Tableaus build down regardless of suit or color; empty tableaus are never filled. The foundations begin with aces and build up in suit to kings.

FORTRESS

Chance of winning: 1 in 10 games.

Deal the entire deck in two wings of a tableau. Each wing comprises five rows, an upper row of six cards and four rows of five. Overlap the cards in each row so that only one card at a time is available. The usual method of dealing is by columns. Move the four aces, as they become available, to a column between the wings. Build these foundations up in suit to kings. On the tableau, build in suit, either up or down as you please. (You may build up on one row and down on another.) One card at a time—the uppermost card of a row—may be lifted from the tableau to be built on foundations or other tableau rows.

In a variant, CHESSBOARD, the foundation-starting card may be chosen. After dealing the tableau, look it over and decide on the rank of your foundations according to what will best promote manipulation of the tableau.

CLOCK

Chance of winning: 1 in 100 games.

Deal the deck into thirteen piles of four cards each, face down. Traditionally, the piles should be arranged like a clock dial—twelve packets in a circle, the thirteenth in the center. In any event, the piles must be considered to be numbered from one to thirteen. Turn up the top card of the thirteenth pile (the center of the clock). Put it face up under the pile of its own number, jack counting as 11, queen as 12, king as 13, ace as 1. For example, if it is the six of clubs, put it under the sixth pile, the pile at "six o'clock." Turn up the top of the six pile and put it under the pile of its own number. Continue in this way, putting a card under a pile and then turning up the top of that pile. If the last face-down card of any pile belongs to that pile, turn next the face-down card of the next pile clockwise around the circle. The game is won if all thirteen piles become changed into fours-of-a-kind. It is lost if the fourth king is turned up before all other piles are completed.

GRANDFATHER'S CLOCK

Chance of winning: 3 out of 4 games.

Take the following cards from the deck: ♥ 2, ♠ 3, ♦ 4, ♣ 5, ♥ 6, ♠ 7, ♦ 8, ♣ 9, ♦ 10, ♠ J, ♦ Q, ♣ K. Put these cards in a circle corresponding to the hours on a clock dial, with the ♣ 9 at 12 o'clock and the rest in sequence around the circle. These are the *foundations*. Build each foundation up in suit until it reaches the number appropriate to its position on the clock; jack represents 11, queen 12, king 13, and ace 1. The sequence of rank is continuous, with ace below two and above king. Deal the rest of the deck into five rows of eight cards each to form the *tableau*. Overlap the rows to form piles of cards spread downward. The top card of each tableau pile is available for play on a foundation or on the top card of another pile. On the tableau, build down regardless of suit. A space made by playing off a whole pile may be filled by any available card.

MISS MILLIGAN

Chance of winning: 1 in 20 games.

Use two 52-card packs. Deal the whole deck in rows of eight cards to form the tableau, overlapping the rows to form piles of cards spread downward, and pausing after each deal to play what you can. Move the eight aces, as they become available, to a foundation row. Build them up in suit to kings. The top cards of the tableau piles are available for play on foundations and on each other. On the tableau, build down in alternate colors. All cards at the top of the pile, in correct suit and sequence, may be lifted as a unit to be built elsewhere. A space made by clearing away an entire pile may be filled only by an available king. After the whole deck is dealt, any available card or build may be lifted from the tableau and set aside as a reserve, of which all cards are available. After these cards are built back into the layout, on foundations or tableau, you may similarly set aside another available card or batch of available cards. You may continue this process until the game is won, or until there is no legal move remaining.

EIGHT OFF

Chance of winning: 2 out of 3 games.

Deal eight tableau piles of six cards each, overlapping so that all cards are visible. The remaining four cards are dealt to four of eight storage cells. There are four foundation piles that build up in suit from the ace. Tableaus build down in suit. Top cards of tableaus are available for play on other tableaus, on foundations, or on the storage cells. Any card may be played to an empty tableau (some play that only kings can be so played, a more difficult version to win). An empty storage cell can hold any card, but each can hold only one card at a time; such cards are available for play on tableaus or foundations.

ACCORDION

ACCORDION *is designed for the player who wants to know his fate in a hurry with no dilly-dally. The pack is dealt out, and there's an end on 't: You win or you don't, almost always the latter.* Chance of winning: 1 in 100 games.

One regular pack is used. Deal cards face up, one at a time, in a row from left to right. Whenever a card is of the same suit or rank as the card at its left, or as the card third to its left, it may be moved over onto that card. For example, if your first four cards are ♠ J, ♦ 6, ♣ 3, ♠ 3, the ♠ 3 may be moved onto the ♣ 3 or the ♠ J. One move may open up others. For example, if you start ♦ 8, ♠ A, ♥ K, ♠ 8, move the ♠ 8 onto the ♦ 8 and then the ♠ A onto the ♠ 8.

Occasionally you have a choice in the order of several moves, and in this case you try to reduce the number of piles as much as possible. You win the game, ha! ha! if you get all fifty-two cards into one pile.

GOLF

GOLF *has scope for a fair amount of skill, and it makes one of the best double solitaires where the packs are not actually amalgamated.* Chance of winning: 1 in 20 games.

Use a regular pack. Deal a row of seven cards face up. Then deal four more rows on the first, making thirty-five cards in all. Overlap the cards so that you can read all indexes. This is the *tableau*.

The rest of the pack is the *hand*. Turn cards up one by

one from the hand, putting them face up in one *talon*. You may go through the hand only once.

The object of play is to clear away the tableau, by building all the cards into the talon. One card at a time may be moved from the top of a tableau pile, if it is in sequence with the card on top of the talon. The sequence may be up or down. For example, if the cards uppermost in the layout are 6-7-8-7-6-5-4, they may be moved in that order onto the talon if it shows a 7 or 5. Suits are ignored. The ace is low and the king high. You may build 2-A-2, but when you have a king on the talon you may not put a queen on it—the sequence ends there. Occasionally you must refrain from playing off all possible queens and jacks from the tableau, saving some for kings not yet uncovered there.

The analogy with golf is that your score is the number of cards left in the tableau after you have run through the hand, and the lower, the better.

Double Golf

Two may play Golf as a double solitaire, each playing his own game with his own pack, by comparing scores at the end. Or they may play nine "holes" for lowest cumulative score. In this case, if a player clears away his entire tableau, any cards remaining in his hand are "minus strokes," and the number is deducted from his total score. Another scoring for the nine-hole game is to give one match point to the winner of each hole separately, and five match points to the lowest cumulative score.

FORTY THIEVES

FORTY THIEVES *is also known as* NAPOLEON AT ST. HELENA, *as it is supposed to have been the pastime with which the emperor beguiled his last exile.* Chance of winning: 1 in 10 games.

Shuffle two regular packs together and deal a row of ten cards face up. Deal three more rows on the first, making 40 cards in all. Overlap the cards toward yourself so that you can read all the cards. This array is your *tableau*.

The aces are *foundations*. Each time an ace is released, move it into a row above the tableau. Build up on the aces in suit and sequence until you reach the kings. The game is won if you succeed in getting all the cards on the aces.

You may remove one card at a time from the top of a tableau pile, putting it on a foundation, or in a space, or on another pile if it is of the same suit and next-lower to the card on top of that pile. For example, the ♥ 5 may be placed only on the ♥ 6 on another pile. Any time you get a space in the tableau, you may use it to release cards from other piles, rearrange builds, and may fill it if and when you please by a card from the hand.

The sixty-four cards left after the deal are the *hand*. Turn cards up from the hand one by one, going through it only once. Play what cards you can on foundations or tableau. Put the ones not immediately playable in a single *talon*, overlapping so that you can read them. You have to keep track of duplicates, because it is not always advisable to make a move merely because you can. Usually you must plan from the beginning how you are going to make your first space, and this may involve not covering certain tableau cards you will need later.

The top card of the talon may be played off, releasing the next below. In the usual course of events, the talon strings out to great length before you get your first space, and then you have to plan carefully just how to dig back into the covered cards.

As in many other solitaires, kings are a nuisance. Until they can be built on foundations, kings can be moved only to spaces, which are then difficult to recover.

SPIDER

SPIDER *is considered by many to be the best of solitaires, for it gives greatest opportunity to overcome the luck of the deal by skillful play.* Chance of winning: 1 in 3 games.

Shuffle two regular packs together. Deal a row of ten cards face down. Deal three more rows on the first, squared up, making forty cards altogether. Then add one more card on each of the first four piles at the left. Finally, deal a row of ten cards face up on the piles.

This layout is your tableau and foundations together. The object of manipulation is to get thirteen cards of a suit on top of a pile, ace uppermost, and running in sequence from ace up to king as you go down the pile. Each time you have assembled a suit in this order, you may lift it right off and throw it out of the game. You win if you get all eight suits assembled.

On the tableau piles you may build down, regardless of suit or color. For example, the ♣ 7 may be placed on any eight. Of course when you can you try to follow suit, but it is more important to get all face-down cards into play as quickly as possible. Each time you clear all the face-up cards off a pile, turn up the next card. If you clear away a pile entirely, you have a space, and that is worth its weight in gold. You may put any available card or group of cards into a space. The only way you can get kings off, other than by assembling complete suits on top of them, is to move them into spaces. But don't be too hasty about doing so, for such spaces are the hardest to recover later. Spaces are needed to interchange cards among tableau piles so as to get suits together.

The top card of a pile is always available to be transferred elsewhere. Also, all cards in proper sequence and same suit as the top card may be moved as a unit. For example, if the top several cards are ♥ 6, ♣ 7, ♠ 8, you may move them only one at a time. But if they are ♥ 6, ♥ 7, ♥ 8 you may move one, two, or three together.

Each time your manipulations come to a standstill, deal another row of ten cards face up on the tableau. Before doing so, you must fill all spaces. Then go to it again. After using up the entire pack, and making all the moves you can, that's the end of it—you either win the game or start another.

A sample beginning: The face-up cards in the layout are:

The first thing to do is to build the "naturals," those that follow suit. You have only one natural play, the ♥ Q on the ♥ K. The card you turn up is the ♠ 4. That gives you another natural; put the ♠ 3 on it. You turn up the ♠ A.

Next move any card that can go on either of two others, so that you may later move it again to make way for a natural, should the opportunity arise. Put the ♠ J on the ♥ Q. Should the ♥ J turn up later, you can move the ♠ J over to the ♣ Q to make way for it.

The ♣ 8 turns up. Now you have only nonnatural plays left. Make a guess, and try the ♠ 7 on the ♣ 8. The ♦ K turns up and you bemoan your bad luck in guessing! But at least that brings off the ♣ Q. Make this move at once, on the general principle of moving higher cards before lower. The ♥ 7 turns up, at present useless. The remaining play is to move the ♠ 4-3 onto the ♣ 5. The ♦ 9 turns up and now play is at a standstill. Deal another row of cards.

NESTOR

Chance of winning: 1 in 10 games.

Deal six rows of eight cards each, face up, overlapping the cards to form eight piles spread downward, and leaving a *stock* of only four cards. Do not put two cards of the same rank in the same pile; if, during the deal, a card turns up that duplicates a card already in that pile, place the duplicate on the bottom of the pack and deal the next card instead. Place the four cards of the stock face up below the layout.

The top card of each pile is available, as well as the four cards of the stock. Discard available cards in pairs of the same rank, regardless of suits. You win the game if you get the whole pack paired up in the discard.

PYRAMID

Chance of winning: 1 in 50 games.

Deal 28 cards in seven rows in the form of a triangle to form the *tableau*. Start with one card in the first row, two in the second overlapping the first, and so on, ending with seven cards in the last row.

Turn up cards one at a time from the *hand,* placing those cards which cannot be used face up in a *talon* pile. The top card of the talon, a card just turned up from the hand, and any *uncovered* cards in the tableau are available to be matched.

Two cards match if they total 13, counting aces as 1, jacks as 11, queens as 12, and other cards their face value. Any two available cards that match are removed together and discarded from play. Kings, counting 13, are removed singly whenever they are released in the tableau or turned up from the hand. You win the game if you clear away all cards of the tableau. There is no redeal.

LA BELLE LUCIE

Chance of winning: 1 in 10 games.

The *tableau* is formed by dealing the whole pack face up in trios of overlapping cards in any convenient array. All cards should be visible. The last card of the pack is single.

Only the top card of each tableau is available for use at any time. On the top card of a pile may be placed the next lower card of the same suit. Aces are removed as soon as available to form the foundations. These are built up in suit and sequence to the kings.

When no further moves can be made following the first deal, the remaining cards in the tableau (not the foundations) are gathered, shuffled, and redealt as at the beginning. When play once again comes to a halt, there is one more redeal.

After the third deal, any one card (called the *merci*) may be pulled out and played. This is almost always necessary to win the game, since a single king above a lower card of the same suit in the same pile will otherwise defeat the player.

GAPS

Chance of winning: 1 in 20 games.

Remove from the pack the four twos, placing them in a column. To the right of each two deal a row of twelve cards, not overlapping, thus using the remainder of the pack. Then remove the aces, creating four gaps.

Into each gap move the next-higher card of the same suit as the card to the left of the gap. The object of the game is to complete one entire suit in each row, in proper sequence from two to king. The catch is that no card may be moved into a gap at the right of a king.

Continue filling gaps as they are created, until all are blocked by kings. Then gather all the cards not in proper suit and sequence with the twos at the left ends of the rows (do not remove the twos). Add the aces to the cards so gathered, shuffle, and redeal so as to fill each row out to thirteen cards. Once more remove the aces and fill gaps as before. Two such redeals are allowed.

CALCULATION

Chance of winning: 1 in 5 games.

Remove from the pack any ace, two, three, and four. Place them in a column. You will try to build these foundations up as follows, regardless of suit:

```
A, 2, 3, 4, 5, 6, 7, 8, 9, 10, J, Q, K
2, 4, 6, 8, 10, Q, A, 3, 5, 7, 9, J, K
3, 6, 9, Q, 2, 5, 8, J, A, 4, 7, 10, K
4, 8, Q, 3, 7, J, 2, 6, 10, A, 5, 9, K
```

Turn up cards from the stock one at a time, placing each turn-up either on a foundation or on any one of four wastepiles placed below the foundation cards. It is best to keep these wastepiles spread downward, so that all cards may be seen. However, only the top card of each pile is available for play and only to the foundations (not to another wastepile). There is no redeal.

Hint: It is advisable to reserve one wastepile for kings, since they can only be removed by completing a foundation sequence.

CRIBBAGE SOLITAIRE

Cribbage Solitaire depends upon Cribbage (page 19) for the scoring. Shuffle a regular pack, then deal three cards to your hand, two to your crib, and three more to your hand. Look at your hand and lay away two cards to the crib. Turn up the next card of the pack for the starter, and score your hand. Then turn up the crib and score it. Discard the eight cards used, place the starter on the bottom of the pack, and deal again. Continue in the same way until you exhaust the pack. At the end there will be four cards left; turn them up and score them as a hand, without a starter.

Count for "his nobs" and "his heels" as usual, except in this last hand.

The object is to make as high a total score as possible in going through the pack. Average is about 85, so that you may consider that you win the game if you make 121.

POKER SOLITAIRE

POKER SOLITAIRE *rewards both lucky guessing and accurate calculation of odds.*

Shuffle one regular pack and deal twenty-five cards one by one, placing them in a 5 x 5 square. The skill arises in picking the best spot for each card. The object is to make as high a score as possible, counting each row and column as a Poker hand and scoring as follows:

Straight flush	30
Four of a kind	16
Straight	12
Full house	10
Three of a kind	6
Flush	5
Two pairs	3
One pair	1

The hands are not ranked as in Poker, but in accordance with their relative difficulty in the Solitaire game. A straight is hard to make, for if you play for it you risk making nothing at all or merely 1 for a pair. A full house is easier, for you can afford to play for it, scoring 6 or 3 if you fail. Flushes are very easy to make; in fact, the usual plan is to try for flushes in the columns and full houses or fours on the rows. Most of the time you will make three or four flushes without giving up any higher-scoring opportunities.

SPITE AND MALICE

A competitive solitaire game for two players, also called CAT
AND MOUSE.

PLAYERS. TWO.

CARDS. Each player uses a regular pack of 52. The rank
of cards is normal, with kings wild. Suits are irrelevant.

DEAL. Twenty cards are dealt face down to each *pay-off
pile* and a further five cards are dealt to each player as his
hand. The remainder of the cards are placed face down
between the players to form the *stock*. The top card of each
pay-off pile is turned face up and placed on top. Whichever
player has the higher card showing will play first. If they
are equal, both players shuffle their pay-off piles and turn
up a new top card. At this stage the center stacks and side
stacks are all empty.

PLAY. The object of the game is to be the first to get rid
of all the cards in one's pay-off pile by playing them to the
center stacks. Only the top card of a pay-off pile is available
for play at any time. Each player in turn may (1) play an
ace to an empty center stack or play to a center stack the
next higher card than the card showing; this card may come
from the hand, from a side stack, or from the top of the
pay-off pile; or (2) play a card from the hand face up on

top of one of his side stacks, thus ending his turn. A player cannot have more than four separate side stacks at one time; if a player has no empty side stacks he must discard on top of an existing stack, thus making the card covered temporarily unavailable for play. The player may make as many plays to the center stacks as he wishes, but as soon as he plays to a side stack his turn ends. One cannot play from a pay-off pile to a side stack or move a card from one side stack to another or move a card from a center stack to anywhere else. If during his turn a player plays all five cards from his hand, without playing to a side stack, he immediately draws five more cards from the stock and continues playing. If a player completes a center stack by playing a queen (or a king representing a queen) his opponent shuffles the completed stack into the stock, creating a space for a new center stack, and play continues.

KINGS. Kings are wild and can represent any card. A player can discard a king to a side stack without committing himself as to what it represents. When a king is placed on a center stack it represents the next higher value than the card it covers.

GAME. The game ends when someone plays the last card of his pay-off pile to the center. The game can also end if the stock runs out of cards, in which case the result is a draw.

RUSSIAN BANK

RUSSIAN BANK *(also called* DOUBLE SOLITAIRE *or, in French,* CRAPETTE*) is a double solitaire in which the two play alternately. The moves are governed by strict rules of order, the penalty for violating which is to lose one's turn.*

PLAYERS. TWO.

CARDS. Each player uses a regular pack of 52. The two packs should have different backs, so as to be readily sorted after a game.

RANK OF CARDS. In each suit the cards rank: K (high), Q, J, 10, 9, 8, 7, 6, 5, 4, 3, 2, A.

PRELIMINARIES. One pack is spread face down and each

player draws one card. Lower card has choice of packs and seat, and has first turn. Both packs are then shuffled thoroughly.

THE LAYOUT. Each player counts off twelve cards (some play thirteen cards) from his own pack and places them face down at his right. This packet is his *stock*. Next he deals four cards face up in a column extending from above his stock toward his opponent. As shown by the diagram to the right, the two columns should be separated so as to allow for two additional columns between them. The eight face-up cards commence the *tableau*.

Each player puts the undealt remainder of his pack face down at his left; this is his *hand*.

THE CENTER. The space between the columns of the tableau is the center. Each ace, the moment it becomes available, must be placed in the center, after which cards of the same suit may be built upon it in sequence from two up to king. The first rule of order is:

I. *If an available card can be moved to the center or upon a center pile, this move must be made before any other* (except as in Rules II and III).

From the tableau depicted above, the first player must move the ♦ A to the center, then build the ♦ 2 upon it.

THE STOCK. After making all possible plays from tableau to center, in his first turn, the player must next turn the top card of his stock face up.

II. *A player must begin every turn after his first with at least one card face up on his stock.*

With regular play, there is always a card face up on a player's stock when he ends his turn. But if he commits an irregularity, it may happen that he is stopped at a time when no card is face up on his stock. In such case he must begin his next turn by exposing a stock card.

III. *On moving the last face-up card from his stock elsewhere, the player must immediately turn another card face up.*

Rules II and III are the only exceptions to Rule I.

IV. *If the stock card is playable upon a center pile, tableau pile, or tableau space, it must be so played before a card is turned from the hand.*

If a space in fact exists, the stock card must eventually be moved into it. But it is not a violation of Rule IV to refrain from making a space when possible. In fact, it is legal (and good tactics) to spread the tableau cards to fill all spaces, so as to get a look at the card from hand, before deciding about the stock card. (Some play that a space may be filled from the tableau, the stock, or from the hand, thus allowing the player more strategic control.)

TABLEAU-BUILDING. Cards may be built on the tableau piles in descending sequence and alternating color: red on black, and black on red; a six on a seven, queen on a king,

etc. Available for building are cards from stock, hand, and
other tableau piles. One card at a time may be moved off
a tableau pile (the whole pile cannot be moved as a unit).

When any of the eight tableau piles is cleared away, a
space exists. The space may be filled by any available card
(subject to rules of precedence), including the top card
from any tableau pile.

The foremost object of tableau-building is to create
spaces so as to get cards off one's stock. But Rule I must
be borne in mind: If an uncovered card is playable to the
center, it must be so played; it may not be kept in the
tableau to facilitate building. Furthermore,

V. *When moves to the center are possible from both stock
and tableau, the move from the stock must be made first.*

THE HAND. When the top card of his stock is unplayable
(meaning among other things that all eight tableau spaces
are filled), the player may turn up the top card from his
hand. If this card proves unplayable, it is placed face up in
a *wastepile* next to the hand, and the player's turn ends.
Should he inadvertently place it on the wastepile when it
is in fact playable, his turn ends nevertheless the moment
his hand quits the card.

If the card from the hand can be played, the player must
then attend to any other plays thereby opened and having
precedence under the rules, after which he can turn another
card from his hand.

After his stock is exhausted, the player may move the
card from his hand into a tableau space.

A card from the hand should be turned so that the opponent sees its face first.

The top card of the wastepile is *not* available—it can
never be moved elsewhere. After the hand is exhausted,
the player turns his wastepile face down (without shuffling)
to form a new hand.

LOADING. At any time that tableau-building is legal, a
player may get rid of available cards (from stock, hand,
and tableau) by loading his opponent. This means building
on the opponent's stock and wastepile. Such building must
be in suit and sequence, but the sequence may go up or
down or both ways. For example, the ♠ 8 can be placed
on the ♠ 9 and then the other ♠ 9 on the ♠ 8.

Stops. A player may call "Stop!" if he thinks his opponent has violated a rule of order. The players should then discuss and settle the fact, and if the charge is true the offender's turn ends forthwith.

In some circles, a rule is deemed violated if a player touches a card when he is bound first to move another. The usual practice in social play is to permit the stop only after the player has picked up a wrong card.

Scoring. Play continues until one player gets rid of his whole pack—stock, hand, and wastepile—into the center and tableau (and by loading). The winner scores 2 points for each card left in the opponent's stock, plus 1 for each card in the opponent's hand and wastepile, plus a bonus of 30.

IRREGULARITIES IN RUSSIAN BANK

Incorrect builds or plays may be corrected only if attention is drawn to them before the offender has completed a following play. After that the error, such as an incorrect sequence on a tableau pile, stands.

Improperly Exposed Card. If a player turns and sees two or more cards at once, from stock or hand, he restores any card improperly seen and his turn ends.

Stops. When a player violates a rule of order, his opponent calls "Stop!" The offender's turn ends and the opponent may let the incorrect play stand or require its retraction. If it was a play from the stock and is allowed to stand, the offender must at once turn up another stock card. A stop may not be called if the offender has been permitted to complete a following play.

STRATEGY OF RUSSIAN BANK

Though Russian Bank requires little more than close attention, it must be classed as a game of skill because the superior player will almost always defeat the inferior. Careful analysis is often required to make the most effective plays in the tableau, but there are no general rules.

KINGS IN THE CORNERS

Players. 2 or more, best for 4 players.

Cards. Standard 52-card pack. Rank of cards is K, Q, J, 10, 9, 8, 7, 6, 5, 4, 3, 2, A (low).

DEAL. The first dealer is chosen at random and the turn passes clockwise after each hand. Deal seven cards to each player. Put the rest of the cards face down in the center of table to form the *stock*. Flip four cards face up from the stock, and place them North, East, South, and West from the stock pile to start four *foundation* piles. If a king is dealt to any of the original foundation piles, it can be moved to a corner position. The player to the left of dealer will have the benefit of making this move and playing a card from hand to replace the moved king.

PLAY. Players take turns clockwise, starting with the player to dealer's left. At his turn, each player may make any number of the following types of move:

1. Play a card from his hand on one of the foundation piles, by descending order and opposite in color. The cards should be overlapped so that all can be seen. Nothing can be played on an ace.
2. Place a king to start a new foundation pile in an empty space in one of the four diagonal corners of the tableau (NE, SE, NW, SW).
3. Move an entire foundation pile onto another foundation pile.
4. Place any card from his hand to any of the original (N, E, S, W) foundation piles that have become empty.

If a player plays all the cards of his hand, he has won. Otherwise, after he has played any cards he can or wishes to, he must draw one card from the stock and his turn ends. If a player is unable to or does not wish to play any cards, he simply draws one card.

If the center stock runs out, play continues without drawing.

The play ends when someone manages to get rid of all the cards from his hand, or when an impasse is reached where the stock has run out and everyone is unable or unwilling to play any further cards.

SCORING. Each player receives penalty points for the cards left in his hand at the end of play. A king costs 10 points and the other cards cost 1 point each. The game ends when a predetermined target score has been reached by one player. The winner is the player who has the lowest number of penalty points at this time.

SPADES

Spades *is a relatively new trick-taking game that has already attracted a wide following.*

PLAYERS. Four, in two partnerships. (For two-hand version, see below.)

CARDS. The pack of 52. The cards rank A (high), K, Q, J, 10, 9, 8, 7, 6, 5, 4, 3, 2. Spades are always trumps.

THE DEAL. Each player receives thirteen cards, dealt one at a time.

BIDDING. Starting with the dealer, each player in turn bids the number of tricks he expects to win, from the total possible of thirteen. His bid, plus his partner's, constitutes the contract of the partnership. The total does not have to equal thirteen tricks.

A player may choose to bid *Nil*, indicating the intention not to win any tricks. After a player has bid Nil, he discards three cards from his hand, face down, in the center of the table. If his partner has already bid, his partner then gives him three cards from his hand and picks up the three discards; otherwise, partner must wait until after he has bid to exchange.

Before he looks at his hand, a player may bid *Double Nil*, thereby doubling bonuses or penalties, and exchange three cards with his partner as in bidding Nil. If both partners bid Nil (or Double Nil), there is no exchange.

THE PLAY. Eldest hand leads first and may lead any suit except spades, which may not be led until the suit has been "broken" by a spade discard on a previous trick (unless the player has no other suit to lead). Players must follow suit if possible. A trick is won by the highest trump or by the highest card of the suit led. Each trick is kept by the player winning it.

SCORING. The object of the game is to fulfill the contract bid by the partnership. If one partner has bid Nil, his contract and his partner's are scored independently, and then the scores are combined.

Tricks count 10 points each for a partnership if the contract is made, 10 against if it is set. (Negative scores are possible.) Tricks won in excess of the contract count 1 each. A bid of Nil scores a bonus of 100 points if made or a penalty of that amount if set. Double Nil scores 200 points bonus or penalty.

If both partners bid Nil (or Double Nil) the partnership receives 200 points if both make their contracts, but there is no score if either or both are set.

GAME consists of 500 points. If both sides go over 500 points in the same hand, the side with the larger total score is the winner.

Spades for Two

There is no deal. The cards are shuffled and cut and placed face down in the center of the table to form the stock. One player takes the top card from the stock. (Turn to start alternates between the players.) If he wants to keep it, he then looks at the second card of the stock and discards it face down to begin the discard pile; if not, he discards his first card before looking at the second, and then draws and keeps the second card. Both players in turn discard one card and keep one card in this manner until the entire stock has been exhausted, at which point each will have a hand of thirteen cards. The discard is then put aside and not used in subsequent play.

Double Nil must be bid before a player has drawn any cards. In all other respects, bidding, play, and scoring are as in Spades.